TALES of LAW and LAUGHTER

RAJU Z. MORAY

OakBridge

First Edition	April 2024
First Reprint	*May 2024*
Second Reprint	*June 2024*
Third Reprint	*August 2024*
Fourth Reprint	***December 2024***

This anthology brings together
thirty anecdotal stories selected
from the popular 'Adaalat Antics' series
written for theleaflet.in by the author **Raju Z. Moray**
and specially illustrated for this exclusive
print edition by **Farzana Cooper**.
Readers will enjoy a humorous
view of the life of a lawyer from
law college to the Bar and the Bench.
These fictional pen-portraits of
lawyers and judges have
entertained thousands of online readers
and there has been an insistent demand
from readers to collect and
publish this treasury of
comic tales in book form.
This anthology fulfills that demand.

• • •

PUBLISHED BY:
Oakbridge Publishing Pvt. Ltd.
M 35, 1st Floor, Old DLF,
Gurugram, 122001, Haryana, India.
Tel: + 92 124 4305970,
E-mail: info@oakbridge.in
www.oakbridge.in

First Edition April 2024

Cover Concept and Illustrations
Farzana Cooper
email:- farzanacooper@gmail.com
Page Layout & Design
Ashwinkumar Borade (Mum)
email:- ashwiin.borade@gmail.com

Note: These stories were first published as
'*Adaalat Antics*' on theleaflet.in portal.

Printed and Bound at:
Saurabh Printers Pvt. Ltd.

ISBN: 978-9395764759

Price in India: INR 495/-

"Humko maaloom hai jannat ki haqeeqat, lekin
Dil ke khush rakhne ko 'Ghalib' ye khayaal achha hai..."
(Mirza Asadullah Khan 'Ghalib')

Having known the truth of "heaven"
(And all Utopias of that kind)
'Ghalib' says such thoughts are okay
For amusement of the mind...

(Translated by Raju Z. Moray)

DEDICATION

This book is dedicated to two personalities who have inspired and continue to inspire me...

Justice **Michael F. Saldanha** (Retd.)
Raconteur par excellence
From whom I picked up the art of spinning yarns

And

Indira Jaising
Senior Advocate
Who has offered me platforms to publish my yarns and poems without fear for the last 35 years.

• • •

Raju Z. Moray

INDEX

	Title	Page
	Foreword	i
	In Lieu of a Disclaimer	iv
1.	The Canteen Court	1
2.	Banana vs. Banana	9
3.	The Lessons I Learnt	16
4.	Preferential Treatment	24
5.	Our Clerk Bigmani	30
6.	Practical Legal Practice	39
7.	Leave Note	44
8.	Wisecrack	48
9.	Edifice of Justice	52
10.	Red Light	58
11.	Every Dog Has His Day	65
12.	What A Spectacle!	69
13.	Counsel Pet	73
14.	The Big Dogfight	80
15.	Mistaken Identity	87
16.	A Bird On The Bench	89
17.	Justice Bigtalk	96
18.	A Judicial Bully	102
19.	Justice Quickfire	109
20.	Mr. Cheatkar & Justice Vichitre	116
21.	Justice Tricky & Justice Lazy	124
22	Milord's Flyover	131
23.	Where the Bus Stops	135
24.	Judgment Day	140

	Title	Page
25.	Judgment Reserved	147
26.	Sheikh...Whatever	152
27.	A Sweet Gesture	156
28.	The Great Fibber	160
29.	The King of Adjournments	165
30.	A Noble Profession	172
	Acknowledgements	181
	About The Author	184

FOREWORD

by **Indira Jaising**
Senior Advocate
Supreme Court of India

Raju Moray has been an author at *"From the Lawyers Collective"* to The Leaflet, spanning a period of over 35 years, with amazing consistency.

His earlier writings have been published in a must-read book **"Court Jester"**.
The book you hold in your hands **"Tales of Law and Laughter"** is in a continuum with his earlier work.

He styles his pieces *"anecdotes"*.

Now scholars do not respect anecdotes as they do not consider them *"evidence"* backed by surveys and statistics. But every lawyer knows that eye witness evidence is the best evidence in law and what you have are eye witness accounts of the functioning of our courts.

Meant for lay people and lawyers alike, these insights tell you what happens inside a courtroom. Every litigant knows the truth of each of these stories, but a lawyer could have said it only with humor to avoid contempt of court.

This is why you will laugh and cry at the same time while reading these stories illustrated by the well-known illustrator Farzana Cooper. You will laugh more than you cry *(if you are not a litigant)*.

For every lawyer this collection has a ring of truth, the truth which cannot be spoken.

So, what makes Raju's work so special? We all know that in every court room, the Judge is the star of the show, the patriarch, the head of the judicial family, the figure of authority and we lawyers focus our attention on he/she/them for an outcome in favor of our client. But Raju has had the advantage of being a player as also a bystander and here he gives us an account of what a court looks like from a ringside view.

What is special about his work is that he pays as much attention to what is around the court as to the judge, the dogs that walk in and out of the court room feeding their young while we lawyers carry on arguing, arrogant judges and sleepy ones, those who visit brothels and those who pray day and night, those who adjourn cases and those who don't, juniors and seniors and their relationship to each other and much more. These judges are real people with their faults, their addictions. One judge wants his flyover free from dirt and filth while the other wants a bus stop closer to his home and the court is available for that purpose.

You will find here lawyers of this court which prides itself as being the finest in the country bend over backwards protecting the canine species in every court, representing the speechless, satisfied at having performed a public service. You will find the very mighty Municipal Corporation of Greater Bombay more than willing to oblige judges rather than face contempt of court. You will perhaps find those who matter more than the judge, the court clerk whose job it is to ensure that a case is heard or not heard on a given day.

You will learn how to avoid a judge and how to seek her out. The pompous lawyers who know no law but know what to gift at Diwali will also be found loitering around the corridors of this spacious and grand structure called the High Court of Bombay. It's a microcosm of life you will find here.

Retired judges who plan their retirement work while on the bench are to be found all around us, leading to the conclusion that if they are not appointed to any tribunal, they get kicked up to the Supreme Court where they constitute a distinct class to be found gossiping in the canteen about their brother judges but only in whispers.

Raju pays as much attention to the infrastructure of justice as he does to the presiding deity of the Courts. If the stories were not told with such a touch of humanity and humor you would want to cry and hold your head in shame as a lawyer, is it really a *"Noble Profession"* anymore you would ask.

Raju has a problem with me, he says he misses the days of **"Court Jester"** of the 1980s.
But it is not I as his editor who has changed, its times that are changing. I need to protect him against contempt of court or defamation.

There are times when I ask him *"please assure me that the people who you write about here are safely dead before we publish"*
He assures me (and I foolishly accept his assurance) that they are and will not rise from the dead to sue him or me.

And yes, I went to the same college as he did, but alas was not as lucky as him. I did not have any contacts in the canteen committee, I got kicked out of the college for want of attendance but, I am still around in the courts and enjoying reading Raju Moray as I hope you do too.

Neither *"The Lawyers"* of the 1980s nor *"The Leaflet"* of modern times would be the same without Raju Moray's stories and poems.

...

1. I have named the real characters wherever they appear. So please don't try to find real persons in my fictional amalgamations.

2. If you still feel you know the characters in these stories, you are free to meet them but don't ask me to accompany you.

3. In my first book **'COURT JESTER'** I invented the narrator Gobble D. Gook, my alter-ego, who lives in Humbug City which has a high court called *"Humbug Hi"*. All action takes place in a country called *'Fake Country'* whose top court is called the '*Court of Supreme Wisdom*'(CSW). Just because Gook's creator is narrating these stories in first person doesn't mean that his milieu has changed.

4. These stories have a large fan following online. These characters still reside there with multifarious litigants and milords.

5. It is best to meet all my characters in cyberspace or

imagination rather than trying to locate them in (or at) the Bar or on the Bench. For the *"incorrigibles"* who insist on feeling offended by imaginary associations made by none other than themselves, I would respectfully suggest that they unwind with a glass of their favourite beverage in hand.

6. It may help if they simultaneously listen to Gobble D. Gook's favourite song. The more adventurous among them can even attempt to find an answer to the fundamental question posed therein:

"Tujhko mirchi lagi toh main kya karuun?"

- Raju Z. Moray

THE CANTEEN COURT

IN the early eighties, it was not difficult to get admission even in the prestigious *'Government Law College'*, Bombay.

After graduating from the science stream, most students opted for medicine or engineering.

The commerce students were more interested in becoming Chartered Accountants or Company Secretaries.
If they did come to law college they came for the 2-years BGL *(Bachelor of General Laws)* degree.
They did not complete the 3-years LL.B course.
(The 5-years option after 12th did not exist then).

The ones who were forced to take up Arts at the under-graduate level because they could not make the cut for

the other sought-after streams were usually at a loss with the ominous question: *"After B.A., what?"*
Quite a few of these joined law college.
But most had no intention to practice law.
Some just wanted to learn law so that they could steer to the right side of it in whatever business they were planning to do.

Most hostelites joined law college to prolong hostel hospitality and most girls joined law college in those days to give some more time to their parents and relatives to find suitable bridegrooms for them.

They would leave law once they got in-laws.

You may say it wasn't the best time to be a sincere student. If one went by matrimonial ads there were no takers for lawyers.

We werc told that those who were rejected and dejected were fit to be injected into law colleges!
All the glamour one finds now was sorely missing.

Although attendance was compulsory there were hardly any students in most classes.

GLC had a few *"super profs"* who had become legends in their lifetimes.

Their lectures were invariably jam packed.
Many outsiders too attended.
No one really bothered to check the entry.
Who does not like the matinee show to be full?
And GLC was among the best *"theatres"* in the country.
While other law colleges were struggling just to stand up and walk, GLC was running on its reputation alone!

A few students, perhaps with masochistic traits, attended every lecture...the good, the bad and the ugly.

I attended the good ones and spent the balance time in organising or participating in extra-curricular activities of which there was no dearth in GLC.

The GLC canteen was the focal point of local politics. With children of many former and current MLAs and assorted leaders in our ranks, even elections of Class Representatives to the 'Students Union Council' were fiercely contested by *"Students Unions"* backed by major political parties.

The present ruling dispensation in our country was only an *"also-ran"* in the student politics of those days. Congress and the Left ruled the roost.

Marathi manoos was also emerging rapidly with their belligerent *'Vidyarthi Sena'*.

If nothing else it greatly enhanced the students' vocabulary of choicest expletives in the vernacular language.

Everyone's mothers and sisters were remembered frequently.

A few of us who were seriously interested in becoming lawyers, were interning with solicitors firms or practicing seniors...or sitting quietly in libraries.
The interns were learning the real nitty-gritties.
Hence, they usually skipped the lectures.

The incident which I am going to narrate is of one year during that three-year sojourn when all of a sudden it was announced by the Bombay University that students who did not have at least 75% attendance would not be allowed to appear for the exam!

We were all at best in the 30% to 40% attendance category. No doubt we were attending college 100% but as far as classes were concerned, we were the *"out-standing"* ones.

So an emergency meeting was called in the canteen to appeal to the *'Canteen Court of GLC Veterans'*.

These were past students who were permanent fixtures in the GLC canteen. They sat there to talk politics and recruit prospective storm-troopers for their parties year after year. Later on, one of them became a three-term MP from Mumbai. But to his credit I never heard him claim to be able to either make or sell tea.

He did however consume dozens of cups of tea everyday!

The veterans told us not to worry.
Such measures were announced every few years...and they had effective *"counter-measures"* to deal with such situations.

The simple, tried-and-tested strategy used by generation after generation in GLC was to strike a deal with the office-clerk *(we will call him Shri Madatkar)* who was in sole charge of the attendance registers.

Madatkar was a most considerate, helpful and reasonable guy with a pleasant demeanour. If he wasn't an office clerk maybe he would've made a good judge.

The first virtue he possessed was that he never asked for or expected any money for helping out!

All he hoped from a student availing his help to tick mark the attendance squares against his/her name and cover up the deficit attendance was a quarter of *'Khoday's* XXX

Rum' which any student could easily afford in those days.

Saturdays was the day fixed for the transaction of rum giving and deficit forgiving.

Madatkar went home with a sackful of small bottles for the weekend.

Maybe he used them to stock up some private wine shops somewhere.

Our problem too was efficiently solved by this friendly office-clerk.

But one of our batch-mates had never attended a single lecture and was not aware of the strict attendance rule that was being enforced that year.

He was even oblivious of our little arrangement with the friendly clerk Madatkar.

Most unfortunately he was the only one to have missed the proverbial deadline bus.

When he found out, he was distraught.
He begged and pleaded with us out-standing students to help him.

We filed an urgent application before the *'Canteen Court of GLC Veterans'*.
It was decided to make an urgent mention of this genuine case before clerk Madatkar.

Madatkar told the pleaders that this happened all the time and the guilty party may meet him on that Saturday evening with his normal professional charges.

Now, our non-attending friend was let in on the volume of the bottle and the brand of the rum.
He had never been to a liquor shop.
And did not know that 40 bucks was all that was needed for a quarter.
He gave 100 bucks and asked for the stuff.
So he got 2 bottles and 20 rupees back!

Holding the precious brown paper bag with Madatkar's *"professional charges",* our friend met the co-operative clerk as scheduled.

Seeing that there was a double benefit being offered, the happy clerk perhaps imbibed a bottle after he went into the deserted office to do the needful.
They were happy hours after all on a Saturday evening.

After half an hour, a bit tipsy, but smiling all the same, Madatkar came out and announced to our friend:
"Jao! Tumhaara kaam ho gaya!"
Our grateful friend thanked the clerk and left.
He must've slept peacefully that night after a long time.

Just before the exam however, he received a notice from the University's Department of Law asking him to see the Head Clerk there immediately regarding *"the matter of your attendance"!*

Sensing trouble, our friend took a veteran from the Canteen Court along.
This veteran also happened to be an office-bearer of the local unit of a national students union.
His father was a judge to boot!
In short, he was the best person to deal with whatever problem that had suddenly cropped up.

The problem was that it had been discovered during *"scrutiny"* that the ever-helpful Shri Madatkar, having helped himself to the extra fees he had received in kind, had celebrated by giving 100% attendance to our friend.
You would ask, what was wrong with that?

Well, our friend had been marked present by Madatkar in the attendance register even on Sundays and bank holidays!

The canteen court veteran argued well.
He said how is a student responsible?
There is always a presumption that everything was legal and proper.
The mistake, if any, was done by some clerk.
What is the student's fault?

The veteran even offered to get the concerned clerk to put white ink on the disputed squares and initial the *"inadvertent mistake"*.

The Head Clerk in the Department of Law knew the veteran's *"connections"* and wanted to be in his good books.
So the matter was hushed up.

Thus all the out-standing students appeared for the exams and we all did well for ourselves.

Not just our efforts, but also Madatkar's efforts were rewarded.

However, several of our masochistic colleagues who had stoically suffered lecture after unbearable lecture, either flunked or were allowed to keep terms subject to clearing backlog.

What can be the moral of such an outcome?

Of all the courts we have appeared before in our now long careers, there was no court which was as much fun as the *"Canteen Court of GLC Veterans"* of the early eighties.

BANANA VERSUS BANANA

ON my very first day in the Bombay High Court I noticed an elderly woman in the long corridor of the main building carrying a load of case-papers in her hands and a knapsack on her back full of bundles of old documents frayed at the edges.

She was often seen walking in the corridor or sitting on one of the benches in the corridor wading through her papers. With thick glasses, several broken teeth and a ready grin for anyone who looked at her, she was almost like a fixture in the corridor.

But I never saw her inside the courts.

As I walked behind my senior one day she stopped right in front of us and started asking my senior when her case was likely to be finally heard.

My senior told her that final hearing matters hardly ever reached but she must not lose hope and be patient…especially as she was now appearing in person.

Then she looked at me with a twinkle in her eyes and with an impish smile asked my senior:
"Will he take up my case?"

My senior appeared a bit taken aback by her question, but soon they both burst out laughing…after a while we walked away!

Naturally, as soon as that day's work was over and I went with my senior to the Marosa Cafe on Meadows Street for our evening round of cup cakes and hot tea I asked him who that old lady was.

This is her story as was narrated to me by my senior, who incidentally, is a far better raconteur than I am…but has unfortunately not penned his memoirs.

Let me call this lady Mrs. Mary Banana.

She was married to an advocate who we will call Adv. Harry Banana.

He was a pugnacious little fellow with a big ego who practiced mainly in the Small Causes Court but used to sit in the bar room of the Bombay High Court.

Where you sat and with whom mattered in those days.

If one called a client for a conference at the Bombay Bar Association the atmosphere gave the client a big high though his cause may be quite small...and filed in the Small Causes Court.

More importantly, there was no haggling about fees with people who used to suffix Esq. after their names.
The esquires had dignity.

And it was not dignified to haggle over fees in the hallowed portals of the Bombay High Court.
Hence Harry Banana frequented the High Court when he had no matters anywhere else…which was almost daily.

Harry and Mary never got along but everytime they tried to amicably part ways the built-in mechanisms of catholic do-goodery got together to stitch up a truce through the medium of the Church with its assorted parish priests and counsellors.

Matrimonial disputes added spice to the humdrum life of pastors and priests for whom they were a good alternative to soap operas in those early days of black and white television shows full of boring documentaries.

As Harry and Mary were Christians and their marriages were supposed to be made in heaven, the British lawmakers had made it very difficult for Christian couples to sever the holy bond of matrimony.

In those days, cruelty was not enough of a ground for Christians to say goodbye to unendurable alliances.
It had to be coupled with another ground such as desertion, impotence or adultery!
Moreover, the grounds had to be proved.

The *'Indian Divorce Act'* governing Christians then was an archaic piece of legislation which flew in the face of the equality clauses of our Constitution but as it was an issue involving minorities no one wanted to touch it with a bargepole.

Another unique feature was that marriages made in heaven and solemnised in heaven's local bureaus known as churches, could not simply be dissolved by civil courts alone!

One had to petition the Ecclesiastical Tribunals to get such matrimonial bonds *"annulled"*.
After enjoying sex for years one had to satisfy priests that the marriage was never consummated.

If one simply managed a divorce through the civil courts without also getting an annulment through the religious tribunal, one could not get married again in the church.

It was an unbelievable system and quite unbelievably it remained in place for ages.

Harry Banana had had enough of Mary.
And she too wanted out.
Both thought that the other had gone bananas.

It is a natural habit of celibate, sex-starved priests to don the role of marriage counsellors inter alia to enliven their vocation with nuggets of salacious gossip which comes as an essential perk with that job.

When Mary started confessing her problems to sympathetic priests, Harry grabbed his chance and filed for divorce.
Cruelty was always a ground.

Now he targeted his wife with allegations of adultery with her more-than-friendly young counsellor.
All hell broke loose in that matrimonial heaven.

A furious Mary and shell-shocked counsellor decided to fight these allegations tooth-and-nail. *(Perhaps that's how Mary Banana had so many broken teeth)*

The case of *'Banana vs. Banana'* was filed in the Bombay High Court.

There was no Family Court in those days and all cases under the archaic *'Indian Divorce Act, 1869'* were filed in the High Court.

Annulments by collusion were encouraged as they added to the disposal statistics but contested causes were long-term investments for lawyers.

Evidence was recorded by the Civil Courts where contested matters were transmitted.

Then the whole pile was dumped back in the High Court's compound for milords to take a call.
This game could go on for years and such prospects were always music to every black coat's ears.

When *'Banana vs. Banana'* commenced there was just Harry Banana after as the Petitioner in the M. J. *(Matrimonial Jurisdiction)* Petition. Mary Banana and her counsellor were respondent and co-respondent.

Mary had engaged an experienced lawyer to represent her while Harry pleaded his case in person.

Soon it was evident that Harry was no match for Mary's lawyer who ran circles around him in legal arguments.

But Harry knew how to make a small cause big.

He alleged that Mary was having an affair with her lawyer and added him as Respondent No. 3!

The lawyer had no option but to give up the brief.

Over the years, Mary went from lawyer to lawyer and Harry added each of them to the array of co-respondents in his M. J. Petition... there were about a dozen co-respondents by the time a Parsi milord of the BHC heard Harry's petition.

The Parsi milord, who became CJ of BHC later on dismissed all allegations of adultery against good old Mary with a remark that was oft repeated thereafter as part of the oral history of Bombay High Court lore...

Parsi Milord:
"Mr. Banana, all these co-respondents are lawyers and even you have not alleged that your wife is insane.

I can never believe that any sane woman would go anywhere near any lawyer after her experiences with one lawyer like you!"

Though Harry's petition was dismissed with costs, he was directed to pay interim maintenance to his wife in a motion taken out by her.
He had no intention of either paying costs or maintenance.

Thus, Harry Banana did not comply.
Contempt proceedings followed and Harry was sent to jail for wilful disobedience.

He was quite happy to spend six months on a prison vacation if he could avoid paying a dime to Mary.

Harry Banana came out of prison after serving his sentence. His legal head was figuratively bloodied, but unbowed!

Now Mary Banana filed for divorce.
All erstwhile co-respondents covertly helped her on condition that she would not ask any of them to represent her in the proceedings.

She had no choice but to fight her own battle.
That is why she was always in the corridors of the High Court waiting for her case to be taken up by some milord.

I then realised why both she and my senior had guffawed when she had inquired if she could ask me to be her lawyer.

They had remembered the fate of a dozen previous lawyers who were conferred the status of *"co-respondents"* by Harry Banana.

I later learnt that my senior too had been one of them.

THE LESSONS I LEARNT

WHEN my *"seniority"* at the bar was all of eight working days, my senior felt that I was senior enough to be let loose before a learned magistrate presiding over what was known as the *'Killa Court'* to *"take a date"*. In those days that was the only dating we juniors could manage.

The official name of that place is *'Esplanade Court'* and that's where the Chief Metropolitan Magistrate of Mumbai sits along with a few other Metropolitan Magistrates.
It is located near the Azad Maidan close to Victoria Terminus Railway Station, the Central Railway HQ in Mumbai.

In a pioneering gender change operation executed by the powers that be, Queen Victoria became *"Chhatrapati Shivaji Maharaj"*.
Mercifully, *"terminus"*, being neutral, though English, remained unaltered.

We had our chambers near the High Court and the Esplanade

Court is just two bus-stops away.

The elderly junior in the chamber who seemed to be a permanent fixture, had taken it upon himself to pepper me with useful tips almost on a daily basis.

Once he came to know that I was to independently go to Esplanade Court, he told me that our senior would give me 100 rupees to attend to the matter and presume I would cab it to Esplanade Court and back.

The one way fare was just 12 bucks in those days.
So 24 rupees conveyance allowance was for the trip.

He said that if I go by bus, whatever I saved would be mine for keeps.
I asked him *"What if I walked?"*
He said *"You are cleverer than I thought"*
I remember that as it was the first compliment
I received in my career as a lawyer.

Then the elderly junior told me to reach the magistrate's court before the learned judge took his seat and to approach the table of the court associate or *"shirastedar"* as he is known.

He said the upper drawer of the shirastedar's desk would be half open and the shirastedar would not even look at me.

He said a ten rupee note was to be slipped into that half-open drawer for the shirastedar to look at me and ask *"Kaay Paahijey?"* (What do you want?)

Then I was supposed to give him a small chit with the number of our case written on it and tell him that we wished to take a date.

The daily list is with the shirastedar and he would mark our case on it.

Once the learned Magistrate took his seat, the roll call would start and when our case is called out I just have to say *"I am appearing for the accused and I need a short date as my senior is held up in the High Court"*

All this seemed fairly simple and uncomplicated.

My chamber colleague said if I walked both ways I would straightaway make 90 rupees for that one appearance!

He made it sound as if I would strike a jackpot but who was I to complain?

I was just happy to be getting an *"appearance"* before a real judge in a real court even if it was only to take a date. Before this, all my appearances had been in moot courts.

Later on, I learnt that especially for lawyers practicing before various courts and tribunals, like my senior used to do, a *"date taking junior"* was a most valuable asset to possess. Smart juniors were dangerous and to be avoided.

They would insist on reading the brief before going to the court and be ever-ready and willing to start arguing a matter at the slightest opportunity which presented itself, fortuitously or otherwise.

And the unfaithful clients were most likely to tempt smart juniors by approaching them directly for their future cases.

Intelligent juniors did not last.

They learnt the tricks of the trade and left their seniors as

soon as they sensed an opportunity to set up their own shop independently.
More often than not they walked away with some of their senior's clients.

The priceless date-taking juniors, on the other hand, never progressed beyond the date-taking stage.

They were happy to go to the court blank, stay blank and return blank from attending matters.

They made no attempt to either read the briefs or to discuss anything with the client.

They got handsome fixed salaries commensurate with their inertia and utility.

A date-taker did not lie when he mumbled *"I have no instructions"* like a mantra day after day, in court after court.
In short, date-takers were indispensable to successful seniors with a varied and large practice.

My senior chamber colleague had been a *"date-taking junior"* for 30 long years and though weak in health was still going strong in utility.

The moment he realised that I had no intention of being a date-taker, he was overjoyed...and most co-operative in assisting my quick exit.

I was just going to be a guest in the Chambers and would pose no threat or competition to him.

Therefore, he had a vested interest in teaching me the *"tricks of the trade"* as soon as possible and to help me branch out on my own.

Coming back to my first appearance, I did as I was told. But as I had walked, I did not have any change in my pocket. Apart from the 100 rupees note my wallet just had a 20 rupees note to cover food for the day.

I dutifully slid that note into the half-open drawer of the shirastedar.

It had an electric effect.

I had paid double the fixed rate of 10 rupees in my very first appearance!

The shirastedar had a big smile on his face and enquired about me, my senior, my future plans etc.

I was pleasantly surprised.

The shirastedar then conducted a quick tutorial for me.

He told me that since I had given 20 rupees, he would call out my matter first and *"relieve"* me in five minutes. He noticed I was a bit nervous and said he would manage everything.

Soon the usher *(called "pattewaala" locally)* shouted 'SILENCE' and the learned Magistrate walked in.

He was wearing big dark sunglasses. I was just beginning to wonder why when I heard one lawyer ask another: *"Tyanche doley aale ahet ka?" (Literally, "Have his eyes come?")*

What he actually meant was "Is he suffering a bout of conjunctivitis or sore eyes" to be wearing those big, dark glasses?

Another lawyer, seemingly a regular there, replied that this magistrate liked to doze off in the post-lunch afternoon session when concluding submissions in trials would start.

Behind these sunglasses no one could make out whether his eyes were open or closed.
I had learnt something new.

They didn't teach this in Government Law College.
The shirastedar sought the magistrate's permission to start the proceedings for the day.

But the learned Magistrate said:
"Wait, where is that matchbox which was here?"

The ushers and the shirastedar scrambled around looking for it...and finally found it.

They handed it to the magistrate.
For a moment I thought he would now ask for a cigarette and have a smoke.

But he just settled down to use the matchstick as a probe into his ear perhaps to quell an irritating itch.
Then he signalled with his free hand to the shirastedar that the board could start.

The shirastedar cleared his throat and as per his 20 rupee promise called out our case number and my senior's name.

He gestured that I should push through the crowd of assorted black coats and stand right in front of the learned Magistrate.

I did as I was directed.

After that, the shirastedar did not allow me to even

open my mouth.

At breakneck speed he gave the learned magistrate my brief biodata, informed him that it was my first time in court, told him the reason I needed some time, gave him the gist of our case and then even suggested the next date after consulting his diary!

In fact, he had asked me which date I wanted and was now pitching that very same date from his side.
It was a virtuoso performance!
The learned magistrate just nodded and did what the shirastedar had literally ordered.

The shirastedar then told me I could leave and go back to the High Court.

But the Magistrate suddenly said:
"Today is his first court appearance. Let us wish him best of luck."

Many lawyers present in the court then shook my hand and wished me.

I bowed to the learned magistrate and said *"I'm much obliged your Honour"*.

The learned magistrate immediately signaled me to stop.
"You must learn how to address magistrates, district judges and high court judges," he said.

I could not fathom what mistake I had made.
I just apologised: *"I'm sorry your Honour."*

The magistrate continued: Remember young man, in our State only the High Court judges are addressed as *"Your*

Lordship" or *"My Lord",* the District Judges are called *"Your Honour"* and we magistrates are to be addressed only as *"Your Worship."*

"So remember this:
In my court you don't
"Honour" me, you
"Worship" me
Samajla (understood)?"
I bowed again
and said:
"Yes, your worship,
I won't forget this
lesson now."

Thus, I learnt another important lesson they had not taught in Government Law College.

As I exited that heritage building and started walking towards the High Court, I still had the crisp 100 rupees note given by my senior in the pocket of my black jacket! It was mine for keeps...but got spent in a day or two.

The invaluable lessons I learnt that day have nevertheless remained with me till this day.

PREFERENTIAL TREATMENT

IN my early years at the Bar, a regular role I had to play was to get cases adjourned or kept back in case my senior was preoccupied in other courts or legal fora.

On such assignments, much depended on the temperaments of the milords before whom I had to appear.

These ranged from the pleasant and accommodative to the rude and haughty.

It was therefore prudent to be prepared in every case to argue the matter if the request for accommodation was refused.

In those days there was a big, fat, and grumpy milord who usually sat single despite his seniority–probably an indication of his *"popularity"* even with his brethren!

He was mostly very rude and non-accommodative to juniors.

They dreaded appearing before him.

Therefore, when my senior asked me to seek accommodation from him in an important matter, I was not very certain about the outcome.

I voiced this concern to my senior.

He just smiled and assured me that there would be no problem at all before this milord because it was my senior's vakalatnama which was on record.

My senior told me to just go and make the request.
On that particular day, milord was in a particularly foul mood. He was ridiculing the unready and skewering even the ready counsel.

Juniors were condescendingly being ticked off as insignificant or irrelevant.

My hopes of being accommodated by this milord were looking very dim.

In due course our case reached and the court associate called out my senior's name.

I got up, gave my appearance slip and mustering courage made the request for accommodation as directed by my senior.

I was in for a very pleasant surprise.
Milord was a very different person in our case.

He first inquired about me:
When had I joined my senior?
Where had I studied law? Had I read the brief?
Did my client not need interim protection?

With new found confidence I told milord that interim protection was of course required but as my senior was on his legs in another big matter before a Division Bench which was likely to spill over into the next day as well, I was seeking the indulgence of having this case placed before milord on the day after.

Milord said he had read the pleadings and was inclined to grant our client ad-interim protection immediately and in fact proceeded to do so!

He then kept the case after a week and very politely told me that even if my senior was unavailable on that day I could attend and argue the same myself. I could not believe my ears.

Milord's transformation that day was nothing short of a minor miracle!

I was overjoyed to narrate the happenings of that day to my senior after court hours.

He, however, just smiled and took it in his stride.
After this, I experienced a similar thing happening in every matter before that milord involving my senior.

We used to get favourable orders even in tough cases without much exertion.
To me it gradually became evident that for some reason not known to me my senior was the beneficiary of preferential treatment from milord.

It was only much, much later after that milord had happily retired that my senior one day narrated to me a story, which threw a lot of light on milord's benevolent disposition towards all cases involving my senior.

It is a tale which can safely be shared now:
Those were the days when my senior was a young, dynamic, bike-riding criminal court lawyer attached to the Chambers of a top-notch Gujarati barrister who was also a very well-connected politician and power broker in Bombay.

That Chamber had several competent juniors assisting the big boss but as far as police station level interventions were concerned, my senior was the preferred junior and the go-to-lawyer.

It so happened that on a rainy weekend, well past midnight my senior received a telephone call from his senior to forthwith go to a police station and get two detainees out of custody without leaving any trace of their detention on the official record.

The mission had to be accomplished the same night whatever it might cost to do it!
The big boss had already made a few phone calls and co-operation had been assured.

So it would not be a serious problem.
But one had to be very discreet lest some lurking reporter with a cop-connection latch on to the happenings and splash it as *"news"* the next day!

Top secrecy and extreme urgency were of the essence in this assignment.

My senior was used to getting such assignments from the big boss. He got dressed, got on his bike, and was off headed for the police station in question.

At the police station, on a bench outside the interrogation room, he saw two pot-bellied men huddled together with nothing on except their underwear.

Their faces seemed familiar.
But it took him a while to recognise these two gentlemen without their clothes on.

He had always seen them fully clothed in black coats and robes.

Both of them were Sessions Court judges!

They had been picked up as customers in action during a raid on a notorious brothel. Upon seeing my senior they hugged him and broke into tears.

As the big boss himself had already made the necessary phone-calls and pulled the requisite strings, getting them out of police custody was not a problem for my senior...but their clothes were still at the brothel where they were apprehended during the raid.

And their wallets and identity cards were in those clothes. If those fell into wrong hands, it would be curtains for *'Their Honours'*.

My senior, however, very efficiently used his contacts and expertise and organised their safe and timely retrieval.

By early morning, the decently clothed judges were

dropped off at their respective residences with their reputations intact.

While the senior of the two took a cab home, the junior one was too shaken and disoriented by the happenings and was grateful for the offer of a ride home as a pillion-rider on my senior's bike!

As he clung to my senior riding pillion on that bike in the cool breeze of the soothing dawn perhaps some indescribable bond of gratitude was forged.

In due course, it was that very bike-borne judge who got elevated to the Bombay High Court Bench.

While he lorded over everyone else, that special bond forged several years ago was not forgotten by milord in my senior's case. By association, I too benefited from milord's soft corner for my boss.

My senior had got milord out of a tight spot during his hard times. Perhaps milord felt he should repay that debt by showing a soft corner even in our hard cases.

OUR CLERK BIGMANI

A very important person in any direct practitioner's life is his registered court clerk. Without this special breed of conjurers cases can neither be filed nor listed.
I was lucky that I got to work with the best and the worst of them.

After my senior dictated a petition to the steno he only indicated when he wanted it placed before the court.

Proofing, checking draft, fair typing on ledger paper with correct spacing and margins, putting all the exhibits and annexures in order, doing the pagination, getting the paperbook stitched and ready for affirmation, affirming it, lodging in the registry, getting a lodging number, getting the case assigned to a court associate for checking, removing the office objections, if any, raised by the checking associate, getting the case finally numbered and then mentioning it before the appropriate court for circulation on the day indicated by the senior all these were to be done by the clerk and the juniors.

Our clerk himself had four junior clerks as understudies and he occupied a pride of place in the clerk's room.
Let me call him Mr. Bigmani.

In our very first meeting Mr. Bigmani told me:
"I have trained twelve judges".

I was wondering whether he lectured at some judicial academy, when he explained that twelve lawyers whose filing clerk was Bigmani, had made it to the Bombay High Court Bench and one had made it even to the Supreme Court!

Bigmani was a magician in the Bombay HC Board Department. But he needed big money to perform big magic.

He could get affidavits affirmed from associates in the absence of deponents, conjure up cases on the board bypassing the mentioning and circulation process, make our opponents' cases disappear from a judge's board if the boss felt insecure or unsure about a particular judge.

Bigmani seldom failed in his assignments but I propose to narrate in some detail just one instance where our collective efforts almost came a cropper.

We were representing an activist bank officer of Canara Bank who had been an officer-director on the Board of Directors.

He was sought to be departmentally proceeded against by the Bank for misconduct soon after his term as a Director was over for allegedly leaking some sensitive minutes of the board's meetings to his agitating colleagues from the Officers Association.

We had challenged the action mainly on the ground that the *'Officers Service Rules'* did not apply to Directors and hence, his actions as a Director could not be faulted and consequentially he could not be penalised under those rules.

The Writ Petition had been admitted and its hearing had been expedited.

There was also an interim relief restraining the Bank from proceeding with the threatened disciplinary action against the petitioner.

Admitted writ petitions in those days were listed on the final hearing board after 3-4 years, unlike the 10-15 years that the same process takes nowadays in the Bombay High Court.

The Bombay High Court in those days had very good judges like Justice Sujata Manohar, Justice P.B. Sawant, Justice C.S. Dharmadhikari, Justice M.L Pendse, Justice S.P. Bharucha, Justice S.P. Kurdukar and Justice Bakhtavar Lentin to name just a few.

Our petition had been admitted and interim relief had been granted by Justice Kurdukar.

After a few years it got listed at the bottom of the final hearing board before the same judge.

Naturally, my senior and more importantly the senior advocate engaged by us as counsel were keen to have the case finally heard by the judge who had prima facie found merit in our matter.

Unfortunately, the weekly final hearing board was always taken up after the day's urgent admission matters were over.

With a judge like Justice Kurdukar, who patiently heard every matter for admission, it meant that the final hearing board would hardly ever start on many days.

Even if it did, unless one's case was listed very high on the final hearing cause list i.e. within the first five matters, the chances of it being heard during the assignment were quite remote.

Thus, our clerk Bigmani was tasked with getting our matter which had moved only from number 28 to 21 in four weeks on the final hearing board of Justice Kurdukar to make a record-breaking jump into the top five matters listed before that judge.

Bigmani, like a seasoned fixer, first had a discussion with the board-makers.

Everything was done manually those days. Computerisation was still far away in the future.

The board-makers advised that the jump ought to be a triple jump spread over the next three weeks so as not to invite undue attention and set tongues wagging. Thus the matter hopped, skipped and jumped to serial no. 17, 11 and six by the seventh week.

We were watching the board with bated breath...because an assignment typically used to last around eight to nine weeks in the BHC.

Unfortunately, when the hearing board had reached no. 5, the assignments changed.

The single bench writ assignment went to Justice Pendse. He was known as a superfast, no-nonsense judge.

This meant that our case would get called out before him in the first week itself! And that was the last thing our designated senior counsel wanted!

He was extremely diffident about arguing the matter before the new judge.

Even my senior felt that we would lose the case before this judge.

Once again, I was promptly despatched to our clerk Mr. Bigmani.

Now, the assignment was to do exactly the reverse of what had been assigned to him earlier.

He was to either make our case disappear from the list completely, or at least to push our case to the bottom of the final hearing list.

Bigmani once again demanded big money.

But it was worth it as the man was a magician.

Our case, which had crawled almost to the top of Justice Kurdukar's cause list was made to vanish from Justice Pendse's final hearing cause list.

However, our joy was short-lived.
Our opponents mentioned the matter before Justice Pendse very tactfully without blaming anyone.

They simply pointed out that one case had "inadvertently"

not been listed after the change in judicial assignment and the registry may kindly be told to look into it.

It was quite obvious that the respondents fancied their chances before Justice Pendse while the petitioner did not. Therefore, while the former wanted the case to be heard by the judge the latter were hoping it wouldn't.

The respondents' attorneys had their in-house clerks and they were no doubt put to work.

But no one in those days was as big as Mr. Bigmani. Once again, big money changed hands in the board department and in the following week our case did get listed but it was listed at sr. no. 50 which was last on the board!

The problem was that Justice Pendse could easily polish off 10 final hearing cases in a week with judgments after completing his daily urgent admissions board.

This meant that in four to five weeks our case could still be heard!

Sure enough, after four weeks, our case had moved up the cause list to no. 12.

Thirty-eight cases had been disposed of and 38 others from the queue were added behind ours.

The final hearing list usually used to be fixed at 50 by the judge.

It was then that in the following week our clerk Bigmani waved his magic wand again.

On that Monday, our case suddenly slipped down the final

hearing board from no.12 and showed up at no. 48 as if some snake in a *'Snakes & Ladders'* game had swallowed it!

Our arguing counsel was most relieved.
He would not stop singing praises of Bigmani.
Then, on Monday night I got a desperate call in the evening from Bigmani.

"Justice Pendse has listed our case at Sr. No. 1 tomorrow under the caption *'For Directions'*.
Please inform Sir and the Senior Counsel."

I did what he had asked.
Sir and the Senior Counsel must've spent a sleepless night!

The next morning the Senior Counsel did not come to the High Court saying he had fever. My senior too was reluctant to go to Justice Pendse's court that day.

Therefore, I was told to *"attend"* the *"Directions"* matter and simply relay those directions back to my senior. In the courtroom, the respondents were present with their full team.

I was the only one from our side.

Luckily, the petitioner was personally present.
Unluckily, he looked like a cunning, crafty fellow and kept grinning at everyone for no rhyme or reason.

The judge took his seat and our matter was called out.
Although the *"advocate-on-record"* in this case was my senior, he was not present and I was *"holding the brief"* for him.

I said I was appearing and also that the petitioner was present.
I informed the judge that my senior was held up and our

senior counsel, who was engaged to argue the matter, had reported sick.

The judge was looking mighty annoyed but did not start venting his ire on me like many judges routinely vent on juniors nowadays.

He only asked me if I had read the brief.
I answered in the affirmative.

The judge smiled and said he did too!

He said he always watched his final hearing board very carefully and read all matters likely to reach for final hearing. Therefore, he had read our matter and was looking forward to hearing it but instead of moving up it had slipped right down.

Hence he had had it placed for *'Directions'* as he intended to hear the same in that week itself.

He however said we could choose any day out of the next three working days!

He asked me to inform the associate our choice of day after consulting our senior counsel.

Before parting he added: "If your counsel is still sick, please ask the advocate on record to make other arrangements or be ready to argue the case himself. No adjournment will be granted."

Outside the courtroom my senior was anxiously

waiting to know what had transpired.

He was pretty cool about it when I narrated what had happened but our senior counsel was now furious at the *"failure"* of Bigmani.

I tried to tell him that the Hon'ble judge himself watched his board but got shouted at for trying to defend the clerk. Bigmani was unfazed when I told him that the counsel was furious.

"Woh ek number ka darpoke hai.
Apne case ke liye Justice Pendse hee achha hai"

I asked him what made him think that?
He told me that the highly respected senior advocate briefed by the Bank in our matter had lost three good cases in the last two weeks before this judge by trying to act *"oversmart"* and that the judge did not like him much.

On the other hand, our senior counsel's father was very highly respected by this judge.

So in all probability, we would win!
I conveyed Bigmani's analysis to my senior.

He told me to keep it to myself but he somehow persuaded our most diffident and reluctant senior counsel to attend Justice Pendse's court and argue our case.

As you may have guessed by now, we won that case.
Bigmani was right on the money even with his predictions.

PRACTICAL LEGAL PRACTICE

YOU may have heard of the saying: *"The end justifies the means."*

Among the Appellate Side lawyers in the Bombay High Court, that was not just a credo but the standard operating procedure.

And it has stood the test of time.

Today, I shall narrate two anecdotal stories *('Short Cuts' and 'Under Postal Certificate')* which exemplify "Practical Legal Practice" a subject which was never a part of any Law College syllabus but which I, during my early days at the Bar, learnt "on the job" so to speak.

* ******* *

SHORT CUTS

Once an appellate side lawyer was representing 123 promotees in a service dispute involving their inter-se seniority vis-a-vis direct recruits.

The parties were desk officers in State Government service and were seeking promotion to the next promotional cadre as Deputy Secretaries.

There was urgency in the case as a status quo order was being sought by these promotees to thwart the direct recruits stealing a march over them in fixation of seniority in the promotional cadre.

However, there was a major problem.

Only around 90 out of the 123 petitioners were available in Bombay to sign the *"vakalatnama"* of that lawyer.

Others were at that moment in different towns of Maharashtra. And there was no time available to ensure their attendance for signing.

So this lawyer *(we will call him "Adv. Jugaadu")* very coolly sent his clerk to get some assorted use-and-throw ball pens in different ink colours from a nearby stationery shop.

They just cost a rupee each in those days.

Then he called out to a bunch of juniors who were hanging around in the Appellate Side Bar Room and requested them to take any pen of their choice and sign against the missing names of his 23 petitioners, who were currently unavailable.

Everyone used different pens and scribbled the names of the missing petitioners as indicated and dictated by Adv. Jugaadu.

Lo and behold!
Within a few minutes, the Vakalatnama was fully signed by all the *"petitioners"!*

The writ petition was quickly readied, filed and the status quo order as desired was obtained in the nick of time.

Later, Adv. Jugaadu explained to the juniors who had ably *"assisted"* him in that important matter that such *"short-cuts",* though normally undesirable and ethically wrong, were all in aid of a good cause.

He explained that such short-cuts were justifiable in emergency situations.

Far from complaining, the beneficiary petitioners whose *"signatures"* were affixed in this manner, were in fact extremely grateful to those who had *"helped"* them in getting the status quo order!

Apart from the tutorial in '*Practical Legal Practice',* the reward for the juniors who had helped was the pen they had signed with.

It was theirs for keeps!

I retained mine as a memento for very long.

Maybe it is still lying around somewhere in a dusty drawer full of old memories.

* ****** *

UNDER POSTAL CERTIFICATE

Once a young lawyer needed to prove that he had served the other side by registered post.

But on the other side was a seasoned litigant who had obviously mastered the art of *"managing"* the postmen. They ensured that no proof of service ever made its way back to the sender!

This was happening regularly.

Neither the packet came back unserved, nor the proof of service in the form of an AD *(acknowledgement due)* card.

Frustrated, the young lawyer narrated his tale of woe to Adv. Jugaadu who was acknowledged by all as an expert in all the "tricks of the trade".

Adv. Jugaadu advised the young lawyer to simply stuff a big brown paper envelope with "raddi" *(waste paper)* and attach a covering letter saying "In continuation of my earlier letters to you, enclosed please find the compilation of documents."

Adv. Jugaadu further advised:
"Send this envelope *'Under Postal Certificate'* and watch what happens."

The result was electrifying!

The other side replied with a stinker sent by their solicitors recording that in none of the earlier letters received from the young lawyer was there any reference to or indication of any compilation which was going to be filed.

The indignant reply further stated that "to add insult to injury, only some old newspapers have been dispatched under certificate of posting!"

The young lawyer was overjoyed as he now not only had an acknowledgement but unassailable proof that all his earlier letters too had been duly served on the other side!

He came to the bar room during the lunch break and thanked Adv. Jugaadu profusely.

Adv. Jugaadu just smiled and responded:
"Young man, don't ever forget that all is fair in love and litigation!"

When other juniors came to know of this super tactic taught by Adv. Jugaadu to that junior lawyer, they realised that the best book for junior lawyers is not any textbook or commentary but the unwritten, invisible code called *'Practical Legal Practice'* by that famous non-author Adv. Jugaadu.

LEAVE NOTE

A busy Appellate Side lawyer was spotted by me rushing to the Bombay High Court on one fine Friday at 4.15 pm.

In those days, the courts rose for the day at 4.45 pm.

He had spotted me as well just as he was about to cross M. G. Road and move in the direction of the High Court.

Upon spotting me, he changed direction and almost ran towards me.

Pointing to a Cafe by the roadside, he began insisting that we have a quick cup of tea since he was seeing me after a very long time and would love to have a chat.

As I was through with my cases in court for that day I accepted his ardent request.

I had no idea at that time as to why he was so keen to have tea with me.

I was soon to find out!

It turned out that he did not wish to go to court at that time and needed some excuse to avoid doing so.

His final hearing case was about to reach and he was quite certain that he would be clobbered out of court by the temperamental judge assigned to hear the matter.

Just as we took our seat in the Udupi Cafe his clerk called to say that his case could reach for hearing any minute.

The lawyer solemnly told him:
"I am in a conference with a very senior lawyer. Catch hold of some junior in the court and ask him to request that the case be kept back."

At 4.45 pm the clerk rang back to say that the case had reached at 4.40 pm and had now been kept for hearing on Monday.

The lawyer immediately told the clerk:
"File a leave note for me for the whole of next week. After that the assignments will be changing."

Clerk: *"The deadline for filing leave notes today is over."*

Lawyer: *"Arrey, what are you guys employed for? Give something in the registry and lodge it immediately, don't waste even a minute!"*

Clerk: *"What reason should I write in the leave note?"*

Lawyer: *"Write 'Gone to Native Place'!"*

Clerk: *"Will you come now and sign the note?"*

Lawyer: *"No, I am still in conference with the senior lawyer. You put my signature as usual."*

Then the lawyer, looking very pleased with himself turned his attention to the tea and me.

Though the entire conversation which I overheard was most interesting, I was particularly intrigued by the bit about his clerk forging his signature on that leave note.

I asked him:
"Is it not dangerous to have your clerk signing like this?"

His answer was amazing...
"Sir, on the Appellate Side, this is quite a common practice. We trust our clerks with everything.

Once, when my hand was fractured and I was unable to sign a cheque to withdraw money from my account, my clerk was my real saviour, not any of my relatives! He wrote out a bearer cheque and signed my signature so perfectly that I faced no problem paying off the salaries and office expenses.

Signing leave notes is nothing compared to signing a cheque!"

I must say, I had to agree with him on that last sentence. At that moment, I recalled what a senior Appellate Side lawyer had once told me.

It seems he had opened an account in the HSBC Bank near the High Court building in the name of his wife.

Once, when he needed to withdraw cash, he got his wife to sign a self cheque and took it to the Bank.
But they told him that the signature did not match!

Then he remembered that he himself had signed for his wife when he had opened his account!
So, on the next day, he signed his wife's signature on the cheque...and the cheque was cleared!

Still, a husband forging a wife's signature was nothing compared to a clerk being allowed (and encouraged) to sign for his boss!

I may be a bit old-fashioned and people may feel I do not trust my staff enough, but I must confess I still prefer to sign my own cheques.

Mercifully, with everything going digital nowadays, cheques have almost become redundant.

However, on the Appellate Side, *"leave notes"* are still the lifeline for many lawyers.

WISE CRACK

THE problem with any attempt at a courtroom wisecrack is that it can just disappear in some crack if the judge is not wise enough to catch it!

A kind-hearted, well-meaning but not-too-bright Milord who tried his best not to displease anyone had the habit of saying every now and then:

"You are right. But he is also right.
Now what can be done?"

An enthusiastic counsel appearing for the workmen of Dena Bank in a case challenging some unjustified recoveries being sought to be made from them by their employer was facing a wily opponent who countered every submission.

Milord was blessing both sides with a nice smile and uttering that famous sentence:

"You are right. But he is also right.
Now what can be done?"

Quite exasperated, the workmen's counsel thought that a wisecrack would probably break the monotony and enliven the proceedings.

He looked at Milord, who was dutifully noting down every submission and declared:

"Milord may see from the facts of this case that Dena Bank has become Lena Bank"

There were giggles from many in the courtroom.
Even Milord looked very interested.

But he did not laugh.

Not even a hint of a smile.

He just picked up his pencil and asked in all earnestness:

"Can you please tell me the date on which this name change took place?"

Everyone was stunned that the judge had not understood that it was just a joke!

The smile had vanished from the wise-cracking counsel's face too.

He just muttered:

"Never mind, milord. I was just saying it in a lighter vein"

At this, milord set aside his pencil and asked with a broad grin:

"Oh, was that a joke?

The counsel nodded sheepishly.

But Milord too had probably caught the wisecrack by then. He started laughing as if it was the funniest thing he had heard in a long, long time!

And with that all the muffled giggles again erupted in a well-deserved chorus of laughter.

For the record, the goody-goody milord went as a CJ to a northern State where his *"Now what can be done?"* attitude was much appreciated.

That earned him an out-of-turn promotion to the SC where his accomodative attitude of not having any view different from the senior judges made him the most sought after colleague.

He is now popular as an arbitrator.

The wise-cracking counsel too moved on.

He got designated as a Senior Advocate, shifted to New Delhi and has established a good practice there.

'Dena Bank' did not become 'Lena Bank' but was merged with the Bank of Baroda with effect from April 1, 2019.

No one knows till now
why *"All Fools Day"* was chosen.

EDIFICE OF JUSTICE

THE Bombay High Court building is a Grade-1 heritage structure.

It still looks somewhat majestic.

But anything under the care of the *'Public Works Department'* cannot retain its majestic appearance for long. Constructed in 1878, this edifice of justice was meant to cater to the needs of about a dozen judges, their staff members, and at most a few hundred litigants.

With the efflux of time and exponential rise in population and litigation, there have been numerous additional rooms carved out, passages enclosed, corridors utilised, doors walled up and air-conditioners fixed.

And all this was purely need-based.

Executed on an ad-hoc, unplanned basis with utility rather

than aesthetics in mind. Cables, like serpents make their way through ugly holes made in walls, arches and columns everywhere.

Wooden partitions divide chambers and ante-chambers blocking natural air-flow.

Water closets have been constructed inside every chamber. All these *"amenities"* were added primarily to make the life of milords as comfortable as possible. This story is about a milord who was very strict and no-nonsense.

Sparing none, he used to run through his board at great speed, as he used to come to court, having read every pleading, and was also very quick on the uptake during oral arguments, which he hardly permitted beyond five to ten minutes.

Then he peered through the thick lenses of his glasses at both sides in turn.

That was the crucial moment.

Everyone watched the judge's face for the hint of a smile. Because the side which got his smile was the side which lost its case. On that particular day, this judge was being especially severe on the Municipal Corporation and its errant officials.

The law officers of the Corporation and their instructing officials were at the receiving end of his tirades.

The judge was asking for top officials including the Municipal Commissioner, to be kept present in court for tongue lashing in the post-lunch session. As soon as the court rose for the lunch break, the hapless law officers ran to the

Original Side Library where their tried-and-tested Senior Advocate *(of first choice and last resort)* was relaxing.

They implored him to please come and appear before the fuming judge after the lunch recess as all the Municipal Corporation matters had been kept back.

This was nothing new for the Senior.

In fact, he had already been telephonically requested by the Municipal Commissioner to appear in these matters.
He told the juniors not to worry.

"Jo bhi hoga dekha jaayega" he said with a smile and a wink.

Scene in the Court post-lunch:
Judge: "*Are the guilty officers kept present?*"

Counsel: "*I am appearing for them.*
Why should they be here?
They have other important work to do."

Judge: "*They must be made accountable.*
They are responsible for unauthorised constructions everywhere."

Counsel: "*How, my lord?*
They did not construct them."

Judge: "*Of course not...but they didn't demolish them either.*"

Counsel: "*Whenever there is any complaint, they take action.*"

Judge: "*That is the problem.*

Why should they wait for complaints?
Why can they not take suo motu cognisance and action?"

Counsel: "*Is your lordship suggesting that we just go and demolish anything we feel is unauthorised?*
No notice?"

Judge: "*You must follow the procedure but don't wait for complaints. The moment you see something unauthorised, you must take action."*

Counsel: "*It is not that simple or easy; the culprits often occupy high positions."*

Judge: "*High or low doesn't matter,*
you must not spare them.
We shall empower you with our mandamus."

Counsel: "*If your lordship directs, we will have to comply.*
But where do we start?"

Judge: "*Start from the top!*
Spare no one."

Counsel: "*I am so glad to hear this."*

But I just want milord to verify and clarify just one small thing tomorrow...if milord doesn't mind.

Judge: "*What do you want to know?"*

Counsel: "*I just want to know whether all the additions and alterations in all their lordships' chambers in the High Court have been done by submitting plans, getting the required approvals, and with sanction of the heritage committee?"*

Judge: "*Of course, all these things must have been done.*"

Counsel: "*I am sure, milord, but still I shall get the copies collected from milord's Chamber tomorrow.*"

I shall also instruct the Corporation to undertake a similar exercise in Mantralaya, Sachivalaya and all other Government buildings in Bombay.

As milord has said, we will start at the top and from South Bombay.

Thus, the matter was adjourned to the next day.

When the next day dawned, it was clear that the additions and alterations in the High Court building were done as the need arose according to the diktats of judges rather than requirements of law.

No plans or permissions could be located anywhere.

When the adjourned cases of the Municipal Corporation were called out, the judge's tone and demeanour had undergone a total transformation.

They were conciliatory rather than confrontational.

Judge: *I have asked the Court Keeper and the Registrar to get hold of the sanctioned plans.*
But that will take some time.

Counsel: "*Yes, my lord.*

You may rest assured that anything beyond the sanctioned plan will be demolished as per the order you are going to pass."

Judge: "*Ah, well...there is no urgency.*
We shall see.
Let us keep all these matters after eight weeks."

Counsel: "*I understand milord.*

Do you need me to keep the Municipal Commissioner or any other officer personally present after eight weeks?"

Judge: "*No, Mr. Counsel.*
That will not be necessary."
After this, nothing happened.

Just as super seniors have a habit of disappearing when they are wanted most, all these cases have disappeared from the board.

And as we had heard in fairy tales.

They all lived happily ever after.

RED LIGHT

To reduce the burden on the High Courts, many tribunals gradually came into existence.

Whether they have helped reduce arrears or added to them is a moot question. But they did offer more avenues to the Government to reward retired HC judges for meritorious services rendered from HC benches.

In metros like amchi Mumbai, finding a place to locate any tribunal is a huge problem.

As a result, most tribunals function in accommodations rented either from other government departments, corporations or even from private landlords.

How exactly these locations get chosen is not quite clear but expediency and budgetary constraints obviously trump suitability and convenience.

This story pertains to a period when someone, perhaps with an impish sense of humour chose Falkland Road *(notorious as a red-light area frequented by mill-workers, sailors, and daily wage labourers)* to house the 'Debt Recovery Appellate Tribunal' (DRAT).

Evidently, the decision-makers had not visited the place before selecting and renting it.

The very name *"Falkland Road"* (often mispronounced by cab drivers and commoners as a phonetically similar sounding unparliamentary word) should have rung a bell.

But all correspondence happened and approvals were obtained by citing its new name, viz. *'Patthe Bapurao Marg'*.

Apparently, this gentleman was a poet who penned *"lavanis" for "tamasha"* artistes to sing.

No doubt it was an apt name for this road.

The problems started after the **DRAT** became functional on Falkland Road.

No one knew where it was and if one missed the location even by a single building on either side, one landed at a commercial sex worker's doorstep. Black coats are not unwelcome per se. But when droves of them start descending at ten in the morning when 90% of the residents have just dozed off, abuses were not surprising if one pushed a wrong and entrance door.

As if this location was not bad enough, the Government soon notified the appointment of an about-to-retire school-marmish lady judge of the Bombay High Court to be the Chairperson of DRAT.

Her Ladyship took the location in her stride and started scrupulously attending the tribunal.

As she got down in a spotless white saree from her off-white official car, she exuded authority. Even her car easily stood out on that desolate lane outside the tribunal building.

It was the only red-light car in that red-light area.
For regulars, it became the landmark by which they came to know which of the buildings they should enter if they wished to be spared the expletives.

The facades of all the decrepit buildings in that lane looked alike.

As the DRAT matters involved high stakes and were a lucrative proposition, the HC seniors were quite eager to be briefed in matters over there.

Thus, when the client in our story approached two counsels *(a senior and a junior)* for his matter in the DRAT they were more than happy to accept.

It was going to be their first time before this tribunal. Friends had forewarned them about a severe parking problem in that narrow lane.

So they decided to hail a cab from just outside the High Court to reach the place.

What follows was narrated to me by the junior counsel in this story: It was 10 am and the DRAT started work at 10.30 am.

The client hailed a taxi.

WEL-
CUM
WELCUM
DRAT
STRI
420

Cabbie: "*Kahan jaana hai?*"
Without answering, the client got in next to the driver and the two counsel, in full uniform *(even clutching their gowns)* got into the back seat of the cab.

Cabbie: "*Sahab, kidhar loon?*"

Client: "*Patthe Bapurao Marg*"

Cabbie: "*Woh kidhar hai Sahab?*"

Client: "*Arrey Baba, Falkland Road! Jaldi chalo. Madam time pe shuru karti hai saade dus baje...*"

Cabbie: "*Aap logon ko Madam chahiye toh ye time galat hai Sahab...itney jaldi wahan kuch bhi nahin milega!*"

Client: "*Bakwaas band karo...jaldi karo. Humara matter nikalne waala hai...*"

Cabbie *(smiling knowingly and nodding at the passengers in the back seat)*: "*Naye customer lagte hai...*"

The counsel were wondering why the cabbie was referring to them as *"customers"*.

As the taxi made its way past Musafirkhana and moved towards Kamathipura (*areas with a shady reputation*) it was quite evident to the counsel what kind of place they had reached.

Senior Counsel (to the client):
"Are you sure you've got the right address?"

"Let's ask someone."

So they stopped and asked a Paan-Beedi shopkeeper at

the junction of Falkland Road.

He told them to drive on straight and stop after spotting a white car with a red light.

If they entered the door behind that car, that was where the DRAT was.

The cabbie then dropped them off opposite the car with the red light. His face wore a perplexed look at the sight of a red-light car in the red-light area.

As the counsel got down and began surveying the surroundings, a few pimps sensed an opportunity and accosted them with sales talk.

The counsel hurriedly scrambled into the building and dashed up the stairs to reach the tribunal in time for their matter.

The lady judge, who knew the counsel from the HC, said she was happy to see them and hoped they had no difficulty in finding the place.

The senior counsel politely replied:
"Not at all your ladyship."

"Your car with its red light was our guide."

However, if the car with the red light was missing on some days, many clients and counsel would enter the wrong door and suffered the consequences.

As was to be expected there were many representations. Finally, they bore fruit. The Falkland Road premises were surrendered.

DRAT shifted to another place...which soon caught fire and burnt down all its records.

All this was a long time ago...

The DRAT has now moved right next to the Colaba Fish Market.

The place has an unmistakable stink…even without the clientele and their lawyers.

Clients and lawyers still get mistaken as prospective *"customers"*.

But mercifully only by the fishmongers.

EVERY DOG HAS HIS DAY

I enrolled as an advocate in 1985.
By the end of that year, I had managed, with considerable difficulty, to get employment as a *"junior"* with a High Court practitioner.

This is another story from those early, unforgettable days.

In Court Room No.6 on the Ground Floor of the Bombay High Court, the late Justice M.L. Pendse was presiding. It was his preferred courtroom in those days, especially when he sat singly.

His board was moving at a brisk pace though it was a final hearing board.

Although my senior's matter was quite a long way down the cause list no one took chances with this judge and my senior had warned me to stay put in the court and *"keep a watch"*.

As a junior, one has to go through this phase which I call *"board-watching days"*.

The job basically involves fetching the chosen counsel from the Bar Library or Bar Room and getting him in the courtroom well before your client's case is called on for hearing.

This was a time before the advent of the mobile phone when apart from listening in on the court proceedings juniors could observe a lot of interesting things happening across the courtroom if only they were a bit vigilant.

I relished these opportunities to observe such *"asides"* which the arguing counsel and their assisting attorneys were in all probability too preoccupied even to notice.
For instance, one milord had this habit of tearing off corners from the ledger paper of pleadings in the post-lunch session to use them to remove remnants of lunch stuck between his teeth.

One may call this legal floss!

The concentration with which he undertook this activity, one wished he had expended on the intricacies of any matter before him.

Another milord of our HC, who retired as the CJ of another HC, used to tear out a longish strip of ledger paper from the outer margin of whichever page of the pleading was open before him at that moment, roll it into a fine hand-made earbud and dig away at the wax in his ears, as if to emphasise the seminal importance of *"hearing"* in his court.

We had heard about litigants having to come to the court with clean hands but here was a milord who probably believed in hearing matters with clean ears too!

Alas, such amusing *"observations"* are increasingly difficult now a days as anyone not "on his legs" in a courtroom is inevitably glued to the cell phone screen oblivious of all the quirky things happening around.

Thus they miss such unforgettable gems.

Well, coming back to Justice Pendse's courtroom on that day.

A counsel who was arguing a matter noticed three puppies come out suddenly from under the raised dais on which the Hon'ble judge sat. After a while, the mother of those pups, after traversing the back corridor entered the courtroom through the door reserved exclusively for the Hon'ble judges.

The arguing counsel's attention was thoroughly distracted by this unanticipated intrusion.

It was evident that he was now concerned more about the dogs than the case at hand.

Then the bitch lay down in a far corner and started suckling her pups.

All this, right there in the court!

The counsel lost focus and started staring intently at the dogs and their activity.

Justice Pendse, unflappable and undisturbed as usual,

just glanced once towards the scene as if it was an everyday occurrence and turning his attention back to the brief and the counsel inquired with his characteristic smile: *"Is there some problem Mr. Counsel?"*

Counsel: *"Milord, the pups are being fed by their mother right here during the working hours of this Court"*

Judge *(looking surprised)*: *"So what has that got to do with this matter you are arguing?"*
"Don't tell me you want an adjournment on this ground?"

Counsel: *"I am finding it very difficult to focus today milord. Could we take this matter up tomorrow?"*

Judge: *"That mother is doing her job. The pups are doing theirs...and I am doing my job. Why should you be reluctant to do yours?"*

That settled it once and for all, there and then. The hearing continued...

And perhaps some precious judicial time was saved from going to the dogs!

WHAT A SPECTACLE!

THIS is a story about a lazy milord of Bombay High Court who often used to enter the courtroom looking thoroughly bored and stifling a yawn.

He belonged to a distinguished legal family from Nagpur and had shone at the Bar resulting in a super fast-tracked elevation to the Bench.

Somehow, the Bombay lawyers failed to impress him and he always appeared to be uncomfortable on his seat. Not that he was not intelligent.

He was.

Evcn had a fine sense of humour.

But a sort of ennui seemed to have taken over.

The routine stuff dished out by the same old chefs of the bar, day-in and day-out, was obviously becoming unpalatable to milord.

He did various neck exercises, shifted around a lot in his

chair and constantly contorted his face making it difficult for counsel to understand whether he was paying any attention at all to any of their submissions.

This incident belongs to that restless period.

Milord had become quite senior and was heading a Division Bench.

Once, an aged lawyer with all white hair was arguing an appeal for admission.

Milord stopped fidgeting and began staring at the lawyer very intently.

All of us sitting in the courtroom waiting for our cases, were very pleasantly surprised to witness the intensity of attention so uncharacteristically bestowed upon this aged lawyer's arguments by milord.

Though senior in age, this lawyer was not a *"designated senior"*.

His case too was nothing out of the ordinary and the arguments were pedestrian.

The case deserved admission and perhaps a status quo.

But we could not understand what milord found so interesting so as to continue this hearing blocking the rest of the board.

Even leaders of the bar and designated seniors had never received such attention from milord!

Such matters took a maximum of ten minutes before this

Bench. Encouraged by the rapt attention however, the old lawyer kept formulating the same submission in various ways for more than an hour before the DB, adjusting his specs and reading from the voluminous paper-book of the case.

The junior milord now started looking impatient. But his senior brother on the Bench seemed engrossed and kept looking at the old lawyer throughout...without interrupting him even once.

So the poor junior milord had no option but to sit patiently and wonder what the senior milord found so very engaging in these submissions.

Finally, the ageing lawyer, clearly out of breath, got exhausted.

He had completed repeating all his submissions and the senior judge appeared to have heard every submission with the same unwavering concentration every time.

It was time to stop.
Hence, the old lawyer finally wound up by saying...

"That's all Milords!..unless Milords have some query?"

At this stage, the senior milord gave a big smile and said...

"Yes, I have a query.

All along I have been admiring these new spectacles you are wearing.

I was waiting for you to stop...
so that I could ask you..."

Lawyer: "*Ask me what, milord?*"

Senior Milord: *Where did you buy these specs from?*"

The old lawyer then proceeded to give milord the details of the shop.

Milord was very happy.

Lawyer: "*Milords, what about my Appeal?*"

Milord: "*Ah! Your Appeal...I almost forgot...yes, admitted.*"

"*Hearing expedited. Parties to maintain the status quo.*"

As lunch break was just half an hour away, the Bench rose early...

We, who had waited since morning,trooped out dejected...having realised that the spectacle of prolonged hearing which we had just witnessed was because of a pair of spectacles!

COUNSEL PET

IT sometimes happens that a milord who is otherwise obnoxious in behaviour selects a particular counsel as his pet.

He then starts bestowing his kindness and blessings in the form of favourable orders upon that counsel.

For the purpose of our story we can call that milord *'Justice Irascible'* and the counsel, *'Counsel Pet'!*

Counsel Pet starts getting a lot of work in the court of Justice Irascible. And as a logical consequence of the judicial munificence of milord, Counsel Pet's fees sky-rocket.

The guarantee of success makes everyone loosen their purse strings and bet on the winning horse without any questions being asked.

Solicitors too make a beeline with briefs to engage Counsel Pet before Justice Irascible.

Counsel Pet then sits mainly in that milord's court from morning to evening and is seen appearing for one side or the other in every other matter.

As milord's seniority ascends, so do the Counsel Pet's fortunes. In due course, Justice Irascible becomes senior enough to start heading Division Benches.

At this stage, Counsel Pet starts quoting such astronomical fees that only parties and attorneys having very high-stake matters can afford to engage his services.

Since the results are a foregone conclusion, tongues of some sour-grapes gowns start wagging at the Bar.

They allege and insinuate that a good part of the fees charged by Counsel Pet must be ending up in Justice Irascible's pockets.

But even those who spread such rumours rush to engage Counsel Pet if they get half a chance in a high stakes matter before the Bench headed by Justice Irascible.

Even though this is an open secret at the local Bar, it is well protected by the *"insiders"* from the *"outsiders"*.

It is not just a matter of guarding a trade secret but also a matter of maintaining the honour and dignity of the Bar.

I daresay that may be one of the reasons why our trade is self-described as a *"noble profession"*.

As a result, many *"outsiders"* who have a good case on

merits, innocuously engage competent lawyers to argue it and expect justice to be done by milords.

Especially as they look so learned and are perched so high. However, they still end up on the losing side.

The insiders who know the reasons smile, but won't tell. The outsiders who don't know, weep but won't know.

The guardians of ethics know everything but observe their own little Omerta. In sum, God is in his heaven...and all is right with our world.

This is a story about how I once got inadvertently involved in engaging Counsel Pet.

It was on a rainy Friday evening many years ago.
On my way back from the Bombay High Court (BHC),
I happened to meet a lawyer whom I knew well, in the local train.

He did visit the BHC occasionally but practiced in many subordinate courts as well.

He was looking very disturbed.

I inquired from him the cause of his discomfiture.

He said that he had a very good case going on for a final hearing before Justice Irascible but that milord was totally against his client.

He said his counsel was being hauled over the coals for no rhyme or reason by Justice Irascible.

He said the hearing in the case was almost over and on

Monday milord had threatened not just to dismiss it but also to impose heavy costs on my friend's client.

Listening to his woes I presumed it must be because milord's Counsel Pet was appearing on the other side.

I asked my friend who was appearing against him.

He named a competent counsel.

Not milord's pet.

I asked my friend what were the stakes.

He said it was a property matter and the real estate involved was very valuable.
Thus, for his client, the stakes were really high.

Then I asked him if he was ready to engage another counsel to appear before Justice Irascible on Monday.

My friend said that the argument of the other side was almost over and milord would probably begin dictating the judgment against his client on Monday itself.

I then let him in on our little *"insider secret"* and told him to contact Counsel Pet immediately and agree to pay him whatever fee he demands.

No haggling, no bargaining.

My friend shared this *"intelligence"* with his client who gratefully agreed to grab this unexpected lifeline immediately.

The very next day my friend met Counsel Pet in his Chambers.

After making a big fuss initially due to the stage the case was at, he agreed to appear in the matter the moment he heard it was before Justice Irascible.

Later on, my friend filled me in about what had transpired thereafter.

As soon as the matter was called out on that Monday, Counsel Pet got up and said that he had been briefed to appear in the matter for the Petitioner and needed some time to study the case properly.

Despite protestations from the other side, time was immediately granted by Justice Irascible.

Thereafter, the tables turned.

The hitherto winning side was lambasted for misleading the court and my friend's side had finally emerged victorious.

My friend was most grateful to me for the *"tip"* and said he couldn't thank me enough.

I was happy that I was able to share what in fact was an open secret of our bar with someone who surprisingly had not heard of it!

After a couple of months, I bumped into another colleague at the bar after a long time and we decided to chat over a coffee break at a local cafe.

After indulging in the usual bar gossip for some time, my colleague told me this:

"Can you believe what happened to me some time ago in Justice Irascible's court?

I had a respondent's brief and as the petitioner had not engaged anyone dangerous, I too engaged a middle-level counsel who was doing a surprisingly efficient job before Justice Irascible.

The final hearing matter was called out in the post-lunch session on a Wednesday and Irascible was completely against the petitioner and fully with us on all issues.

On Friday, just before the court rose for the day, he even indicated in the open court that he would dismiss the petition with exemplary costs.

Me client and I were relaxed and pleased with the way things had gone for us.

But something deadly happened over the weekend.

Counsel Pet suddenly appeared for the petitioner on Monday and Justice Irascible, not surprisingly, took a complete U-turn!

As a result, we ended up losing a case which we were on

the verge of winning!

Now our only hope is the Apex Court."

My colleague continued: *"The petitioner's lawyer was obviously tipped-off by some insider from our Bar who knew Justice Irascible's magic equation with Counsel Pet. That ruined everything for us. Our bad luck I guess."*

I guiltily gulped my coffee down.
Then I lunged forward and picked up the bill as soon as it arrived on the table.

You may say it was my way of atoning for the *"sin"* of letting an *"outsider"* in on one of the closely guarded open secrets of our Bar.

Justice Irascible has retired.

As expected, he is making merry in arbitrations.

Counsel Pet, who made his millions during the reign of his chief benefactor, invested wisely, got a senior gown, and does not need to practice in courts anymore.

He says he now prefers arbitrations.

Our profession has kept its nobility intact.
And our Bar is still rated as one of the best in the country.

THE BIG DOG-FIGHT

ONCE upon a time, the Brihanmumbai Municipal Corporation (BMC) used to catch stray, unlicensed dogs, keep them in dog-pounds for a few days and thereafter euthanise them if they were not claimed and rescued by anybody. It was no doubt an extremely cruel way to treat man's best friend.

But that was soon to change in the late nineties. Spurred on by animal welfare movements all over the world, and led by vocal activists like Maneka Gandhi in our own country, the BMC decided to opt for the more humane method of sterilising the stray dog population in Mumbai instead of exterminating it.

In 2001 the Union *'Ministry of Culture'* under Maneka Gandhi, passed the *'Animal Birth Control (ABC) Rules'* for stray dog population management.

With most government departments having gone to the dogs,

it was heartening to see the Ministry of Culture framing rules for protecting stray dogs.

An *'Animal Birth Control' (ABC)* Program was formulated under the aegis of the *'Animal Welfare Board of India'* (AWBI) and several Non-Governmental Organizations (NGOs) sprung up rapidly to implement it.

They were to be paid an incentive by the AWBI per dog they sterilised.

This was a different kind of *"nasbandi"* and there was a decent amount of money on offer.

The idea was that in about 10 years there would be no new dogs born and thus the city would be rid of the stray dog *"menace"* once the existing stray dog population died a natural death without being euthanized.

But the *'ABC Program'* soon ran into trouble.

After a few years the BMC claimed that statistics submitted by the NGOs showed that they had already sterilised more dogs than the total dog population as indicated in the dog census commissioned and compiled by the BMC!

There were allegations that several NGOs took credit for sterilising the same dogs and all of them benefited from the funds on offer by adding those dogs to their tally and claiming credit!

All through this period, stray instances of stray dog bites continued to make news.

Puppies too were being noticed at many street corners prancing around certified *"sterilised"* dogs.

People began having doubts about the ABC program and started asking questions.

Soon the *"anti-dog lobby"* started demanding a resumption of the old system of impounding and euthanising stray dogs.

The *"pro-dog brigade"* immediately rose up in defence of maintaining the status quo as per the ABC Rules.

If the arguments of the attackers appeared to be rabid, those of the defendants were no less ferocious.

The media was a fertile battleground for opinions from both sides.

At such a crucial point in the stray history of Mumbai, one senior milord of the Bombay High Court, who was very scared of dogs, was returning on a weekend from a late night party at a friend's place to his official residence when he spotted some stray dogs near the entrance to the judges residential complex.

He alighted from his car and started shooing them away. As he apparently had imbibed a lot of courage at the cocktail party, he was feeling unusually brave.

So he even ventured to pick up a few pebbles and hurled them at the stray dogs to scare them away.

At this, the dogs charged at him and milord was forced to run for his life in the direction of the watchmen's chowky.

Being unsteady on his feet, milord fell down and some dogs caught hold of his trousers.

They ripped them apart.

The watchmen chased the dogs away and rescued milord but he was shaken to the depths of his underpants. More than his body, his ego seemed to have been bruised by this involuntary exposure.

He felt his modesty was outraged and his reputation lay in tatters at least in front of the watchmen.

The next morning, milord dictated a complaint to the Municipal Commissioner and another letter to the Chief Justice narrating his ordeal quite dramatically and faithfully, except for his own inebriation and provocative action.

The Chief, whose grouse had been that the stray dogs blessed the tyres of his car every morning, promptly asked the HC registry to treat the aggrieved milord's letter as a Public Interest Litigation (PIL).

Thus commenced *"the big dog-fight"* before the Bombay High Court.

A division bench issued notice to the BMC on the PIL which inter alia sought re-commencement of the impounding and euthanising of stray dogs to counter their *"menace"*. For the media, this was an ideal, non-controversial, time-pass story.

Readers and viewers love to expend their energies and take sides in such matters.

On the returnable date, there were a dozen intervention applications filed on behalf of the various NGOs and animal-welfare activists.

On the date after that there were half a dozen interventions supporting the PIL and the molested milord.

Meanwhile, another division bench in another case upheld the legality of the BMC's ABC Program and opined that it was a good program which must be given a few more years to show good results.

As a result, this letter-PIL was referred by the Bench to the CJ for constituting a larger Bench as they were of the view that the ABC program was a failure and a total waste of money!

Thereafter, for over a year, the dog-fight cases were heard by a 3-judge Bench of the Bombay High Court.

Both sides had engaged senior advocates but the best Parsi lawyers of the Bombay Bar in those days turned up in the court not to represent the humans on either side, but for the stray dogs!

I used to attend the hearings in court and was most amused to notice a similarity between the dogs and their pro-bono counsel.

No, not the long noses. That was just coincidental.
But the fact that while pleading their case these counsel invariably tended to raise one leg and place it on the adjoining chair. It reminded me of their *"clients"* who habitually raised their legs in a similar manner on lamp posts.

On the big judgment day the senior-most judge on the 3-judge BHC Bench ruled for continuing the ABC program but the two other judges *(which included a lady judge)* felt that the BMC was *"duty bound"* to control the *"menace"* and perform its obligatory duties towards rate-paying citizens.

That was a long time ago.

So did the culling of stray dogs recommence?
No way.

This is the beauty of litigation.
Dogs may come and dogs may go, but the tail of litigation shall now keep wagging forever.

SLPs were filed in the Supreme Court against the 3-judge HC full Bench's split verdict.
Even before the Supreme Court, the Parsi doyen of the Supreme Court Bar appeared pro bono for their *"four-legged friends."*

The SLPs were promptly admitted and the status quo restraining reversion to the old system has continued since then.

The AWBI continues.
So does the ABC program.
The dogs, the activists, and the NGOs supporting them and their counsel are all very happy.

After 25 years, one may say the ABC Program is a partial success.

Strays have not disappeared but their numbers appear to have reduced...at least in Mumbai.
Puppies, if sighted, are quickly being adopted and find good homes instead of wandering on the streets.

If dogs are dying prematurely in this city it may not be due to the dog haters but probably because of too many dog lovers!

When I see open packets of unconsumed Parle-G biscuits lying in front of every fat, bored, sleeping dog at Churchgate Railway Station I realise that it is this diet, coupled with hardly any exercise that is likely condemning these stray dogs to an early exit from Planet Earth.

Some day, no doubt justice will be done.
But as things stand, it doesn't seem likely in the lifetime of these overfed stray dogs or their supporters.

MISTAKEN IDENTITY

THIS was narrated by a senior advocate from the Bombay High Court who retired as a Supreme Court judge. In the good old days before life became digital, everything was basically physical.

After having consented to being considered for elevation to the BHC Bench, it was a given that the IB would do a background check to ensure that there were no skeletons lurking in some cupboard of the candidate. So our senior advocate, who lived in a nice house with a garden was tinkering in his garden on a weekend in a lungi and banian, when he spotted two suspicious looking gentlemen staring at the house.

He ignored them at first but soon realised that he himself seemed to be the object of their attention and subject of their conversation.

After a while, they approached the advocate.
"Tum idhar ka maali hai kya?"

The advocate just smiled.
The investigators did not wait for an answer.
The muddied banian was evidence enough.
Without much effort they had struck gold and were happy about that.

Pulling out a notebook they began questioning.

"Kitne saal se kaam karta hai yahan?"
"Ye tumhara Sahab kaisa aadmi hai?"
"Kuch lafda-wafda toh nahin?"
"Kabhi daaru peeke danga karta hai kya?"

The interrogation lasted about 20 minutes and the informant maali was most co-operative as by now he had spotted the regulation brown shoes these cops were wearing and surmised the purpose of their visit.

He assured the cops that the *"Sahab"* was a decent man.

Having satisfied themselves that no maali would speak in such glowing terms about his employer, unless that gentleman was truly honourable, the two cops even offered a small tip to him, which of course the maali dutifully declined.

After a few days the *"maali"* was appointed a High Court judge.
The rest, as they say, is legal history!

A BIRD ON THE BENCH

THE sight of a senior counsel weeping at a farewell brought to mind another instance of weeping I had witnessed in my early days at the Bar.
It is worth narrating.

For the first 50 months at the Bar I was a junior of a well-known lawyer who was an Assistant Government Pleader (AGP) for the State of Maharashtra on the Writ Cell attached to the Bombay High Court.
Many such AGPs, including my senior, got elevated to the Bench in due course.

That Writ Cell in those days was a hub of frenetic activity. Mingling almost daily with the 50-odd people manning that office in the late eighties *(from peons, stenos and office staff to the Superintendent and the AGPs)* for 50 months was, to say the least, not just an invaluable, but an unforgettable experience.

This long apprenticeship gave me unimaginable insights

into and access to the strategies *(and sometimes shenanigans)* of the State and its lawyers.

It also stood me in great stead when I set up my own independent practice.

The AGPs were permitted private practice as long as the State was not involved as a contesting party. Many used the convenience of a rent-free space in the High Court complex to cultivate their private practice.
They handled just the bare minimum required cases for the State which ensured an extension of their tenures.

The tears I witnessed were from a person who had come to meet an AGP soon after it was announced in the newspapers that the AGP's name had been cleared for elevation to the BHC and that his warrant of appointment was due any day.

As I had come to know the AGP very well I had gone to his cabin. He sat me down for a chat and offered me a cup of tea.

Random people whom I did not know kept dropping in, wishing him, shaking hands and walking away.

I kept trying to leave, but the AGP said I should continue sitting otherwise one of those visitors would occupy the chair and not leave!

After a while, the court reporter of a leading newspaper came to meet this AGP.

He too was invited to sit and join for tea.
I knew him well too.

We were happily chatting away when a man looking

distraught and holding back tears barged in without knocking, and said loudly:

"Sir, ab humara kya hoga? Aap humaare mai-baap ho!" (Sir, now what will happen to us? You are like our parent)

Then, noticing me and the reporter, he backed off.
The AGP signalled him to wait outside.

The reporter scented a story!

Another AGP walked in to wish the would-be judge.
The reporter and I used this opportunity to exit the cabin.
Outside, we saw the same man who had barged in.

He was weeping profusely.

The reporter walked up to him, patted him on the back and asked him why he was so upset?

The man said: *"Ye sahab humare liye bhagwaan ke barabar hai. Ab woh judge ban jaayenge toh humara kya hoga?" (This sahab is like a God to us. Now, if he becomes a judge, what will happen to us?)*

This was the *"peg"* which the reporter wanted!

He did not need to hear anything more.

He took my leave and rushed off to write his story.

The warrants too arrived late in the evening and the AGP was now officially to be sworn in as a milord.

The story of his elevation, as narrated by the reporter, was splashed prominently in a leading newspaper.

It described how despite a very lucrative private practice, this lawyer devoted much time to the thankless task of being an Assistant Government Pleader.

The reporter then wrote about the *"poor clients"* of this AGP who would be *"orphaned"* by his elevation.

And he adroitly used the quote: *"Ab humara kya hoga?"* to narrate how he had unexpectedly encountered just such a weeping *"client"* in the AGPs office.

The human-interest angle in that story inter alia ensured that the AGP's first sitting upon elevation was with a very senior milord handling a plum assignment.

I went back to the usual hustle-bustle of life as a junior assisting my senior in juggling between his private practice in various subordinate courts and his job as a senior AGP in the Writ Cell.

One fine day I saw the weeper in the Writ Cell again. I noticed that he was desperately pleading with the Superintendent and the Assistant Superintendent.

These two officers were the fulcrum around which life in the Writ Cell revolved.

The Superintendent and his Assistant Superintendent wielded tremendous powers and all the AGPs tried their best to keep them in good humour.

The Assistant Superintendent had become a good friend of mine.

After that weeper left, he walked towards me and said that he desperately needed to smoke and have a cup of tea in the canteen and requested me to tag along.

What I learnt from him threw a new light on the cause of the weeping which I had witnessed a few days earlier.

No reporter would ever have guessed the cause.
Nor had I.

It seems that the AGP who got elevated had managed, with political clout, to get instructions issued to assign all *"Forest Act matters"* to him.

With the *'Environment Protection Act'* just having come into force, many permissions for felling of trees by contractors had been denied and existing licences had been revoked.

Naturally, the contractors had all rushed to the High Court with writ petitions challenging such actions.

Everything would depend upon how the State Government responded to their pleas.

The man who was weeping was the biggest wood-cutter of them all!

He had apparently struck a deal with the Forest Act AGP to take a fall, like they do in WWF wrestling matches. An unheard of amount had exchanged hands.

The AGP had *"co-operated"* in getting all similar cases clubbed together before one Division Bench.

But just as the bunch of these matters was due to be listed, the news of his elevation to the BHC bench was announced.

The contractors had already parted with the full amount. So there was nothing that they could possibly do, but weep!

This was the *"real"* story behind what I and the reporter had witnessed on the day the warrant of appointment of that AGP was to arrive.

The reporter had got it all wrong.
And had ended up projecting a venal man as a hero!

I asked the Assistant Superintendent why the weeper was pleading with them now?

He said the *"contributors collective"* wanted to know if there was any chance of getting back their contribution from the AGP who was now a milord.

I was most curious to know his answer.

The *"wisdom"* he imparted to me that day was amazing. Certainly not something one is taught in any law school.

He said he and his boss, the Superintendent, had told the weeping man that the contractors must always remember that there is honour among thieves.

Thus, they must simply be patient and let the AGP get confirmed as a permanent judge.

Thereafter, their bird on the BHC Bench would be worth thousands in the forest!

JUSTICE BIGTALK

THEY say that the new generation does not buy books. They say that the culture of reading books has diminished, if not vanished. And they point to libraries being empty and bookshops shutting down.

They have a point.
But their assumptions are not entirely correct.

The reading habit has not decreased but increased. However, most people are reading off screens rather than from paper books. Digital is being preferred to physical chiefly for convenience.

Not only is there paucity of space but e-books are much cheaper than paperbacks and supposedly more environment friendly.

It is in this scenario that the physical paperback books made a huge comeback on the pavements of Mumbai.

These are simply unauthorised copies of all the latest bestsellers.

But of late they are so well-produced that they often look better than the originals, thanks to the use of advanced digital technology and better quality paper by the book pirates.

These books are typically sold at 20% of the MRP of the same books in original, legal editions. As a result, pirated versions are often cheaper than the official Kindle Editions.

The area around the Bombay High Court is teeming with pavement booksellers. Placards proclaiming *"Pick Up Any Book for Rs. 100"* are common. And all the latest bestselling books are freely available in pirated editions.

There was a time when the official publishers would lodge complaints and pressurize the authorities to conduct raids and seize the pirated books.

Now they seem to have thrown in the towel.

Some big publishers had even moved the HC seeking a mandamus to the law enforcement authorities to activate in practice the laws lying dormant on paper.

As it happens in such matters, apart from delivering homilies and sermons to the authorities and asking them to initiate action, precious little was achieved.

The milord who heard that piracy case, however, got a lot of publicity in the media during those days. And as a result, he was invited by a few law colleges and rotary clubs to lecture on the *'Menace of Piracy'*.

We can call him Justice Bigtalk.

I happened to attend one such lecture as a friend who was a professor at the law college had been quite insistent that I attend.

And what a lucid lecture it was!

Justice Bigtalk, who was a Ph.D. in something, held forth to the students on how piracy was a big crime as it involved theft of intellectual property of the creator of the artistic work.

He pointed out how the poor authors got nothing, the publishers got nothing and only the copiers were making money!

He ended his lecture by making the audience *"pledge"* that henceforth they would never buy anything except a legal copy of any book.

The students gave him a standing ovation.

Bigtalk went home pleased with himself.

About a month after this great event, I happened to be in the Fort area on a non-court-working Saturday.

Many lawyers do come to their chambers on such days when the courts are closed to attend to miscellaneous work.

We always dress in coloured casuals on such days.
It is a refreshing break from our usual black and white or shades of grey.

Most of the pirated book sellers used to be second-hand books sellers earlier and preserved that stock of old books in case they were warned of a raid by their friendly sympathisers.

Then they simply displayed those old books and hid the pirated ones. The 100 rupee placards were replaced by 20 and 50 rupee ones!

I love to browse through such old books on pavements as one can often discover some old classic or out-of-print edition at a throwaway price.

On that Saturday, as I was indulging in this familiar weekend activity, I noticed a gentleman in a bright red T-shirt and blue denim jeans haggling with my friendly bookseller about the price of some books he had picked up.

This is how the conversation progressed:

Customer: "*Hum teen kitaab lega. Bolo kitne me dega?*"

Bookseller: "*Sahab pirated books mein kya milega? Sirf 100 mein de rahey hai. Official price 499 hai.*"

Customer: "*Tumko maloom hai ye illegal hai?*"

Bookseller: "*Sahab, hum kahan zabardasti kar raha hai? Aap dukaan se le lijiye. Woh MRP pe 20% off denge.*"

Customer: "*Agar wahan se lena hota toh mai idhar kyun aata?*"

Bookseller: "*Sahab aap kitna dena chahte hai?*"

Customer: "*Hum teen kitab ka 200 dega!*"

Bookseller: "*Nahin parwadega sahab.*
Humko bas 10 rupaye milte hai ek book ke peeche..."

I was finding this conversation most irritating because on the one hand this customer was talking about legality and then haggling about pirated books!

So I turned to look at him.

And who do you think it was?

He was wearing big dark sunglasses...but there was no mistaking him.

It was Justice Bigtalk!

As I was staring at him with the three pirated books in

his hands, I could see that *"shock of recognition"* on his face too!

When he saw me staring at the books he quickly put them down, turned around and briskly walked away.

I smiled and turned towards my bookseller friend.

He was obviously quite oblivious about the identity of the haggling customer who had vanished so suddenly, but the question he posed spontaneously was quite funny...

"Dekha na sahaab yahan kaise-kaise log chale aate hain?"

I wish the collegiums who select *"kaise-kaise log"* could hear such questions from the street and if possible, provide some answers.

A JUDICIAL BULLY

NOT too long ago, the Bombay High Court had a judge who had been elevated from the Nagpur Bar.

Even his elevation had become a matter of controversy and was delayed for some time as many had made allegations and opposed it.

But this judge was finally appointed.

He was duly confirmed in due course.

After that, he was permanently posted at the BHC's principal seat at Bombay where he served till retirement.

When he retired, he was senior enough to be part of the High Court collegium.

His volatile temperament, nasty remarks and generally

boorish behaviour was detested by the Bar but his ability to clear arrears of backlog by finally disposing even complicated cases argued by batteries of senior lawyers kept him free from harm.

We will call him Justice Irascible.

Many hot-potato cases which other judges had avoided taking up were regularly assigned by whoever was the Chief to Justice Irascible.

He made short work of them in no time with reasoned judgments and orders.

Gradually, the Bar began to tolerate Justice Irascible and accepted him as a package-deal of good and bad qualities.

For some reason, Justice Irascible did not like ladies practicing law. He was openly misogynistic at times.

In one instance, he had insulted a respected lady lawyer who was not present when her case was called out and who later explained that some domestic duties had delayed her a bit that day by asking in open court:

"Why do you at all come to court?
The proper place of women like you is in the kitchen"

As the lady lawyer did not make an issue of it and as social media was unheard of in those days, Irascible got away with the nasty remark.

Personal remarks and insults were a frequent occurrence in Justice Irascible's court. His targets usually were the ones who couldn't or wouldn't retaliate.

Which meant very old lawyers, very raw juniors or lady lawyers.

One could say without exaggeration that Justice Irascible came across as a quintessential judicial bully.

I remember two instances from his court vividly.

They illustrate two different facets of this judge's personality.

Was he suffering from bipolar disorder?
We will never know.

The first instance was when a senior labour lawyer stood up to him.

Judge: "*Is this the way to draft a writ petition?*"

Advocate: "*I am engaged as a counsel.
The AOR may have missed something...though I personally find nothing wrong with this petition.*"

Judge: "*That shows your caliber is extremely poor.*"

Advocate: "*That may be your opinion Milord.
It is not a fact.*"

Judge: "*Do you not know even the basic concepts of writs?
Look at your grounds...your prayers.*"

Advocate: "*Milord may hear me and then decide.*"

Judge: "*Who gave you a law degree?
We must start issuing show cause notices to law colleges and universities which confer such degrees upon people like you.*"

Advocate: "*Milord may kindly hear the matter.*"

Judge: "*No. I want to know. Answer my question. Which University gave you your law degree?*"

Advocate *(after a long pause, looking at the judge straight in the eye): "Milord, it is the same University which gave you yours!"*

That shut Justice Irascible up good and proper.

After that, he quietly heard the matter.
Surprisingly, he even granted reliefs!

The second instance was when a fairly senior Appellate Side lawyer wanted to avoid arguing his matter before Justice Irascible but was wondering how he could possibly dodge this pugnacious judge.

Just then, a young girl who had recently got her sanad *(licence to practice)* from the Bar Council came to the bar room looking for this very lawyer.

She told him that she had been referred by someone and was wondering if he could accommodate her as a junior in his Chambers.

To the lawyer, this was a Godsend.

He told her that he would consider her request but before that he would like to give her a small *"test"*.

She just has to go to a courtroom in a little while and when one case of his was called out she simply had to *"Ask for time"*.

That's all.

The girl, who had not expected to appear in court that very day, complained that she did not even have the proper uniform.

The lawyer immediately requested obliging Bar Room colleagues to loan her bands and a gown, handed her the brief and led her to the door of the courtroom of Justice Irascible. He then instructed her to just go in, sit, and do as she was told.

If she could get an adjournment from the judge she would be employed!

By now, many of the bar room juniors who had nothing better to do than watch what happened in Justice Irascible's court when this unsuspecting girl asked for time, went to the courtroom to watch the *"fun"*.

The girl was not from Bombay.
She knew nothing about High Court practice and procedure but perhaps had some idea of panchayats and talathi proceedings at the village level where all proceedings were in Marathi.

As a result, she displayed no sign of any stage-fright or nervousness. It may be that her ignorance was the cause of the bliss visible on her face.

As she sat in the court waiting for her *"senior's"* case to reach, she kept mumbling *"Ask time, ask time, ask time"* lest she forgot those words.
In all probability, she was sub-consciously doing a quick Marathi translation of what she had to say.

So when the matter did get called out after a while, egged on by the watching juniors, she very boldly stood up.

Judge *(glaring at her): "Are you appearing in this matter?"*

There was total silence from the girl.

Judge: "*What do you want?"*
Once again total silence...

The judge, realising that she probably did not understand English, (to his court associate, in Marathi):

"Tila vichaara, kaay pahije?" (Ask her what she wants)

The associate then conveyed to her milord's query in Marathi.

And the Girl replied:
"Saheb kiti vaajlet?" (Sir, what is the time?)

Now the associate was flummoxed.
So was Justice Irascible, who, by now, looked more bemused than annoyed.

Here was a young girl asking him what was the time!

He then asked her in Marathi. Why did she want to know what was the time.

She replied that her senior had asked her to.

Now, the judge was most curious.
He first asked her when she had got her *sanad.*

She candidly confided that today was the first day she had come to the High Court to meet the senior and that this appearance was to be her *"test"!*

Justice Irascible looked stumped.
He understood her plight and asked her very patiently:
What exactly did your senior tell you?

The girl cheerfully replied:
He told me to come to your court and ask for time.
That is why I am asking what is the time!

At this, even Justice Irascible could not control his laughter.

He told the court associate to grant a brief adjournment in that matter and told the girl that she had passed her *"test"!*

But before parting with the matter he made it a point to tell her that he wanted her senior to remain personally present along with her on the next date of hearing so that she could witness how Justice Irascible was going to *"test"* him!

JUSTICE QUICKFIRE

THESE are some fond memories of a milord who had been transferred to the Bombay High Court from his parent Rajasthan High Court.

For the first few years after his transfer milord's *"head-quarter"* was at Nagpur.
He very quickly made his mark among the Nagpuris as an efficient, no-nonsense judge who would not suffer fools easily and would compel advocates to constantly be on their toes in his courtroom.

Stories of his quick-fire style soon started travelling to the principal bench at Bombay. The lazy worthies of the Bombay Bar thanked their stars that he was firing away at their Nagpur colleagues instead of them.

We can refer to this milord as *"Justice Quickfire"*.
One particular anecdote from Nagpur which attracted a lot of attention in the Bombay bar-rooms in those days was

about the dressing-down he had given to a Government Pleader over there in open court.

The said GP thought no end of himself and usually had his way in most courtrooms of Nagpur.
Those were not the days of Video Conferences but this gentleman's initials were "V.C".

It seems he was arguing in support of some application before Quickfire J. when the learned judge asked him under which provision of the *'Civil Procedure Code'* such an application could have been filed?

Mr. V.C. fumbled.
He had not anticipated this.
He tried to dodge, evade, but Quickfire J. wouldn't let go of him.

Legend has it that it was at this juncture that Quickfire J. uttered these immortal words:
"Mr. V.C. it seems you do not even know the 'ABC' of 'CPC'! "
That did it!

From that day, poor Mr. V.C. literally lost his initials.
From then on, he was ragged either as 'ABC' or 'CPC' in the bar-room!

Thus, when news trickled in that Justice Quickfire was being moved permanently to the Principal seat at Bombay, the Bombay lawyers were not exactly enthusiastic about his arrival.
Some even started reading CPC for the first time since they had passed out of law college!

Now, I witnessed some scenes when Justice Quickfire

settled down in Bombay and started presiding over Division Benches.

Once, a lawyer from a subordinate court was arguing before a Bench headed by Justice Quickfire.
As is the practice in those courts, he kept calling the judges "Your Honour".
(The practice in the High Court is to call them "Milord")

Noticing the sniggers from the haughty Original Side seniors opposing the poor guy, Justice Quickfire turned to them and asked them:
"Are you at a circus?
What is it that you have found funny?"
That froze the smiles on their faces.

Then, turning to the arguing advocate, Justice Quickfire remarked: *"Mister, it seems that High Court practice is not your cup of tea!"*

The advocate, though very pleased that the sniggerers had been shown their place by Quickfire, did not quite understand the import of this question.
He turned to his assisting junior, and inquired: *"Kya poocha judge sahab ney?"*

The junior: *"Sir, woh pooch rahey hai shaayad aap chai pasand nahin karte?"*
The advocate smiled and nodded knowingly. Addressing the bench, he replied:
"No Sir, I prefer coffee!"

You can imagine the laughter which erupted after this! And Justice Quickfire had laughed most of all...

On another occasion, in a matter concerning a claim for

pension by the second wife, a lawyer from a subordinate court was struggling with submissions and Quickfire J. was losing patience.

He kept saying: *"Come to the point mister"*

The lawyer was clearly overawed by the barrage of questions being thrown at him by Quickfire J.

Like a number 11 batsman facing a fast bowler, he missed most of them. But till that point at least he had managed to preserve his wicket.

Finally, Quickfire J. thundered:
"Just tell us the issues involved Mister"

At this, the lawyer's face brightened.
At last he had understood what the judges wanted!

Lawyer: *"Sir, there are only two issues in this case."*

Quickfire J. *(pulling out his notepad and picking up his pencil)*: *"That is good.Tell us..."*

Lawyer: *"Sir, the first issue is from the first wife and the second issue is from my client!"*

Once again, this brought the house down!

Quickfire J. told the lawyer to sit down and passed appropriate orders without any further *"assistance"* from that lawyer.

During every vacation, Quickfire J. would travel to various hill stations in Maharashtra and absorb as much knowledge about them as possible.

As a result, he became extremely well-informed about the places he visited.

Once, while heading an Appellate Side Bench he was hearing a case involving a challenge to some mining permission given near a protected hill fort.

Quickfire J. asked the Assistant Government Pleader:
"Do you know which is the highest peak in Maharashtra?"

AGP: *"I cannot remember..."*

Just then a designated senior entered.
Quickfire turned to him: *"We need your assistance Mr. Senior Counsel."*

The senior was flattered.
Adjusting his square gown, he moved forward.
Quickfire J.: *"Please enlighten the learned AGP about which is the highest peak in Maharashtra?"*
The Senior, obviously expecting some intricate constitutional query, was stumped.

Senior: *"Milord...I have it at the tip of my tongue..but..but.."*
Quickfire: *"But there is no one to prompt you?"*

The courtroom which was packed with many seniors was stilled into silence as Quickfire J. started asking the same question to one after another.

In those pre-Google days, there could be no relief by pulling out the cellphone and using *"fastest finger first"*.

One by one, the seniors started disappearing by exiting from the courtroom very quickly, as if their matters were reaching elsewhere!

They were followed by their entourages.
The courtroom, which was packed a few moments ago, suddenly wore a deserted look.

Some of those who had run out of that court stood outside the entrance to warn others not to enter as a *"General Knowledge Class"* was going on!

Just then, a senior whose roots were also in Rajasthan, entered to appear for the Bombay Municipal Corporation in a matter which was on Quickfire's board where contempt notices had been issued to some BMC officers.

Seeing him Quickfire J. smiled and said:
"You please don't answer"

BMC Counsel *(looking puzzled): "Answer what milord?"*

The poor AGP, who was the original addressee of the GK question, was still on his legs after 15 minutes of the "Class".

He whispered to the senior counsel:
"Lordship was asking everyone which is the highest peak in Maharashtra?"

The BMC counsel smiled: *"Oh! That is Kalsubai...I met milord there during the last vacation!"*

That brought the curtains down on that period.
GK Class was over!

The students who did not know the answer and had left the *"classroom"* returned and sat quietly clinging to their briefs in the courtroom.

MR. CHEATKAR & JUSTICE VICHITRE

IN the days of transition from printed reports of court cases to fully digital reporting accessible on the internet, a prominent law reports publisher from Nagpur had devised a tempting scheme for lawyers.

The publisher offered to load the entire database of case-law reported by their well-known journals covering reports from the Supreme Court of India and various High Courts into the computers of those who would subscribe to the various schemes on offer.

Different permutations and combinations of Civil, Criminal or Labour & Service Laws etc. were on offer.

For the entire database the one-time payment was quite substantial.

Thereafter, for a reasonable annual subscription the company's representative would visit the subscribers every month and use his code to update the subscribers database with the newly added cases for that month.

This is the story of a representative of that famous company who decided to do some unauthorised moonlighting.

We can call that salesman Mr. Cheatkar.

He first visited my chamber soon after the scheme was introduced in the mid-nineties.

All the *"packages"* and *"modules"* he deftly presented were quite attractive.
However, they were priced way beyond my reach at that time.

Each package was in the range of 1.25 lakhs as a one-time down payment and a 25k annual subscription for physical loading of monthly updates by their representative viz., Mr. Cheatkar.

I was impressed by the demo given by Mr. Cheatkar and especially by his friendly demeanour but at the end of that meeting I frankly told him that I could not afford the packages on offer at that stage of my career.

He smiled and replied:
"Sir, you are absolutely right!"

I was surprised.
He continued: *"Most lawyers I met have said the same thing!"*

"So I have come up with a 'special scheme' for all such lawyers from my side."

Naturally, I was eager to know what this *"special scheme"* was.

Mr. Cheatkar said he would install every available database of his company only for Rs. 25k each and upgrade it for only 500 rupees every time!
He made it clear that he was doing this at his own risk as a *"service"* to the legal profession.
Therefore, his customers had to trust him fully.

There would be no contract, acknowledgement or official invoice and the transaction would be strictly and entirely in cash.

In short, he would use the company's *"codes"* and *"keys"* in his possession to unlock the collective wisdom of all legal brains over the years into our computers for a fraction of the official price charged by his company.

Though the offer was tempting, I regretted my inability to accept it.

I told him that I felt it was wrong on his part to be disloyal to his employer company and that I would not be comfortable being a participant in a scheme which was morally *(and legally)* wrong. I told him that in my opinion what he was doing was most unethical.

Mr. Cheatkar looked genuinely surprised.

He told me that he has *"sold"* his *"special scheme"* to over a thousand lawyers till then and I was only the second one among all of them to have declined his offer.
But he said I was the first one to do so on ethical grounds!

I was not at all surprised to know that so many lawyers had opted for Mr. Cheatkar's scheme but I was curious to know from him who was the other lawyer who had declined the offer...and why?

I therefore offered Mr. Cheatkar a cup of tea and requested him to tell me about the first person who had declined his special offer.

He named a very eminent and flamboyant criminal lawyer who was a designated senior advocate.

Apparently, that senior lawyer was impressed by what was on offer and even lauded the *"enterprise"* of this bright young *"Marathi manoos"* as such *"schemes"* had hitherto been the monopoly of Gujaratis and Sindhis!

But the reason he gave for declining the tempting offer was that at his age and seniority, most judges accepted whatever he said was the law, as the law.

With every passing year, he had told Cheatkar, the standard and quality of appointments had steadily deteriorated so much that there was hardly any studious and hard-working milord left on the Bench to challenge whichever submission he made on any question of law!

"I no longer need case-law to win cases. My face law is enough for me" is what he had told Mr. Cheatkar.

As he was leaving my office I once again tried to persuade Mr. Cheatkar to stop being disloyal to his employers and told him that he could get into serious trouble if his *"operations"* ever got discovered.

But Cheatkar said he had all his bases covered.

He had opened a separate account in a small co-operative

bank which had an even more "co-operative" manager in Navi Mumbai and all the cash collected from this "side-business" was deposited safely over there, out of harm's way and scrutiny.

Mr. Cheatkar had then vanished from my life only to resurface once again around six months later.
This time as a prospective client!

His tale of woe is worth sharing here.

It seems in order to hawk his *"special scheme"* in newer areas, he had landed in Seawoods Estate, a posh residential area in Navi Mumbai.

There he noticed a lovely bungalow.
A board proclaiming *"Justice Vichitre (Retd.)"*
hung at the gate.

Sniffing another prospective client, Mr. Cheatkar ventured inside and rang the doorbell.
After a servant let him in, the learned judge himself emerged from his bedroom to meet the visitor.

Cheatkar went through his entire well-rehearsed routine with Justice Vichitre.

Imagine his joy when Justice Vichitre not only appreciated his wares but asked:
"If I want to officially purchase each and every database you have for subscribers, how much will it cost?"

Cheatkar: *"Sir, that would be 7.5 lakhs"*

Vichitre: *"And if I pay you hard cash and don't want any bill ?"*

This was music to Cheatkar's ears.
"I shall unofficially load everything in your computers for 3 lakhs and even update it every month for free!"

Justice Vichitre did not bargain at all.

He asked Cheatkar if he could do the job immediately.
Cheatkar said if he got the cash immediately he could load everything immediately.
Thus the deal was finalised.

Justice Vichitre led Cheatkar into his study and showed him the computers.
As Mr. Cheatkar started working, Justice Vichitre went off to fetch the cash.

Soon, every database of Mr. Cheatkar's company from Nagpur was in Justice Vichite's computer database at Navi Mumbai.
Justice Vichitre treated Cheatkar to snacks and tea and handed him brand new notes totalling 3 lakhs.

As Cheatkar left Vichitre's bunglow he thanked his lucky stars and decided to go home and celebrate.

At this point in his narration Cheatkar angrily exclaimed:
"I want to teach that Justice Vichitre a lesson!"
I asked: *"Why?"*

Cheatkar: *"Sir, on the very next day when I took the notes to my co-operative bank manager friend he checked them and said that all of them were fake!"*

I told Cheatkar that it was possible that someone had given them to the judge and in good faith he had given them to him!
All he had to do was take the fake notes back to the judge and sort out the matter.

Cheatkar: *"Sir, that is exactly what I tried to do but the judge kept dodging me for two weeks.*

Finally, I had to literally barge into his bungalow to gain access to Justice Vichitre!"

"Then what happened?", I asked.

Cheatkar: *"Sir, Justice Vichitre was well aware that those notes were fake. He said he had been cheated by a lawyer just a few days prior to his retirement.*

He had granted bail in a case of murder and this money was given by the lawyer of the accused as part of a "goodwill gesture".

Since he had retired there was no way he could do anything now about being duped!

So he was waiting for a chance to get rid of these notes. Cheatkar had probably rung Justice Vichitre's doorbell in answer to his prayers!

Justice Vichitre also proceeded to give a lecture on ethics and morality to Cheatkar and told him he was free to go anywhere and file any complaint.

He said the result of any such move against him by Cheatkar would only result in a one-way ticket for Cheatkar to jail.

Justice Vichitre gratuitously advised Cheatkar that just as he had passed on the fake bucks to him, he should pass them on to unsuspecting others!

And to top it all Vicitre invited Cheatkar to share a round of drinks saying: "People like us should stick together and collaborate!"

Cheatkar wanted me to help him recover his 3 lakhs from Justice Vichitre.

I told him that he should just write off that amount as there could be no legal remedy in an entirely illegal transaction. Cheatkar was not happy with my advice but realised he had no options.

Several months later, I bumped into Mr. Cheatkar on Dalal Street.

He looked very happy.

I asked him how his *"side business"* was doing?

He replied that it had flourished rapidly and Justice Vichitre was responsible in no small measure in boosting it by his word-of-mouth publicity!

Mr. Cheatkar and Justice Vichitre had become good friends. It seems Vichitre had a round of drinks with Cheatkar every time Cheatkar visited his residence to upload new case-law. For his bosses in Nagpur however, ignorance was bliss.

JUSTICE TRICKY & JUSTICE LAZY

EVERY new Chief Justice who takes charge in any high court of our country promises to do *"something"* to tackle the accumulated backlog of pending cases in that high court.

The fact that all subsequent Chiefs promise exactly the same thing when they arrive on the scene proves that none of their departing predecessors succeeded in fulfilling that promise.

One innovative Chief who had been transferred to the Bombay High Court from Delhi had devised a novel idea to try and speed things up.

For the subordinate judiciary, he introduced a system of awarding marks to every judge based on the number of disposals achieved every month by that judge.

Desirable targets were set and different marks were fixed for different categories with final disposals fetching the highest marks.

For his privileged brethren in the High Court, however, he could do no such thing as He was merely the *"first among equals"*.
Still, he announced that their *"disposals"* would be displayed for study on the official website.

This move yielded a strange result.

The subordinate judges told the lawyers appearing before them that they must somehow achieve the *"quota"* of cases fixed for them.

They candidly proposed that if members of the Bar cooperated with them to cross their targets for the month in a shorter time, all of them could take the remaining days off if they liked!

The Bar loved this proposal as it opened up the possibility of taking mini-vacations every month and availing of massive off-season discounts.

I recall how a friend of mine who was a prosecutor was summoned by the Sessions Judge to whose court he was attached.

As he was waiting outside the wooden cabin to be called inside, he could hear the judge speaking loudly over the phone with a colleague.

This is what he overheard:
"Aaj tumhi kiti udavley?"
("How many have you eliminated today?")

My friend told me later that he felt as if he was eavesdropping on a conversation between two encounter specialists!

In the High Court, when the Chief analysed quarterly charts of disposals as reported by the registry he was shocked to find that the disposals of two of the laziest milords in the High Court who hardly did any work, were far higher than the disposals achieved by those who sat late and worked very hard.

Some of us at the Bar however knew the *"secret"* behind these - *"achievements"*.
There is no harm in sharing them now.

One milord used trickery and jugglery while the other creatively used his inherent aptitude for inertia.
We can call them Justice Tricky and Justice Lazy.

Justice Tricky would prepare a short cause list for urgent admissions every day and a very long one for final hearing matters.

He took up only the urgent admissions board and sat with it for the entire day…and still did not finish it on any day.
He never touched the final hearing board day after day till the lawyers took it for granted that at his speed *(or lack of it)* he would never get past even his daily admission board.

Then, suddenly on one fine day when no one in the final hearing list would be present, he would run through the urgent admission board.
Not by hearing and disposing of the matters, but by adjourning most of them.

Justice Tricky would then start calling out the matters on the long final hearing board one by one.

In every matter, he would pass the same order:
"Parties and advocates absent when matter is called out. Dismissed for want of prosecution. Interim orders, if any, to stand vacated."

This way, Tricky J. notched up hundreds of *"disposals"* in a matter of minutes.
This was dutifully added by the registry to his *"tally"* for the day which was meant for public display.

Thereafter, on the same day or the very next day, all those lawyers whose matters had been called out and dismissed would line up begging Tricky J. to restore their cases to file.

Tricky J. would then lecture them about how those old cases had been pending for years and how they owed certain duties towards their clients.

He never failed to mention how the milords sat beyond hours of duty to serve the cause of justice, but lawyers unfortunately did not reciprocate the commitment of milords and remained absent!

However Tricky J. would be very polite and considerate. He would conclude his little homily by saying:
"I will not entertain any oral requests for restoration. Please take out proper proceedings giving reasons for your inability to remain present."

The lawyers obviously would have no choice but to get that done.

These applications for restoration would then be given different numbers by the registry.

Tricky J. would then list all those matters together.
By a common order, he would then impose nominal costs to be paid to the Legal Aid Authority or the Bar Library and proceed to dispose of all the restoration applications by restoring the dismissed cases back on file for some other milord to hear and decide in due course.
The disposal of the numerous applications for restoration of dismissed matters also served to boost Justice Tricky's tally.

This modus operandi was adopted in different categories of cases throughout the assignment of Justice Tricky to notch up impressive statistics for the Chief.

Justice Lazy, on the other hand, was intelligent but lethargic.

He would take up assignments in direct and indirect tax matters and put all his interns to work to find out cases involving common issues.

He would then ask the counsel concerned to get all such cases clubbed together.

Such lists of dozens of cases were then displayed on the board as *"Group Matters"*.

Then he would ask the competent practitioners appearing before him to pick out groups which were *"covered by SC judgments or earlier HC judgments"* so that those could be disposed of on a priority basis by short common orders.

As this suited the counsel, they even obliged lazy milord by very helpfully preparing draft proforma orders!

In this manner, hundreds of disposals could be accomplished in a few days and they showed on Justice Lazy's report card!

Such *"achievements"* were then compiled by someone in the registry into impressive statistics and supplied officially to whoever wanted to prove that in our High Court the milords, against all odds, were zealously performing a herculean task.

In Parliament, the Law minister answered MPs on the basis of such statistics and newspapers reported such *"official information"* dished out by the bureaucratic number-crunchers. Those of us who felt all this was just an "eyewash" or "jugglery" were not looked upon kindly by the milords who pretended that all was well.

They felt the honour of our great High Court was at stake and it must always be shown in good light, whatever its shortcomings.
So we behaved just like the relatives of a heavily made-up bride behave at her wedding.

The honeymoon, however, is now over.
Among other things, as a result of such efficient *"case-load management techniques"*, the arrears have now reached gargantuan proportions.

But barring a few notable exceptions, most mediocre milords who are guaranteed their salaries, perks and retirement benefits, have no incentive to spoil their eyesight or tax their brains once they take their seats and get confirmed to warm the high benches till they retire.

As one of them, a friend who has now retired from the High Bench, once confided in me:
"If my lethargic brother, incapable of disposing even five cases in a week, is treated on par with some of us who dispose fifty cases, and if he still gets all the same benefits on a platter, why should we bother to do all the work and take all the trouble?"

I wish I had a reasonable answer to my friend's fundamental question.

MILORD'S FLYOVER

ONCE upon a time, the Division Bench of the Bombay High Court which was assigned to hear matters pertaining to the *'Municipal Corporation of Greater Mumbai'* (MCGM) was manned by the two of the most volatile and temperamental milords of the Bombay High Court.

Many considered them to be pompous, rude and overbearing.

The municipal law officers confessed to friends at the Bar that they often woke up in the middle of the night due to nightmares about being tongue-lashed in the court by these two milords.

Entering the court of these two milords was akin to entering a hallowed mansion closely guarded by a bloodhound and bulldog.

The milords of course fancied themselves to be the best watchdogs of the Constitution.

I shall first narrate an anecdote involving the junior milord. The story involving the senior milord can be adjourned for two weeks.

These anecdotes will offer readers a glimpse of what members of the Bar had to face during that turbulent judicial assignment.

Here is the first anecdote.

One day, the junior milord suddenly asked a MCGM counsel:
"Who has put the huge flower pots along the flyover?"
The counsel replied that it was done to beautify the road.

That triggered an outburst:
"Do you guys realise the value of that flyover?

It is the first of its kind in the entire country.
An engineering marvel when it was built.
People from all over come to see it.
One of the finest engineers in India has designed it.
And you dare to spoil and damage it by putting flowerpots on it?"

The counsel,who was not prepared for this lambasting, said that he would surely look into the matter.

Milord: *"We want the Superintendent of Gardens to personally give an explanation.*
Keep him present in court...else we shall summon your Commissioner!
Have you seen the muddy brown water staining that beautiful

black road early in the morning?
And you intend doing this daily!
Ever thought about the additional load these huge concrete pots are imposing on the back of this ageing landmark?
Your people have no sense of aesthetics or beauty.
But we are not helpless.
We are warning you.
Those pots must be removed forthwith!

Next time we are crossing Peddar Road, we don't want to see any of those ugly pots. Such eyesores!

And yes, the flyover must be cleaned thoroughly and restored to its former beauty."

The MCGM top brass knew that to displease a milord on the Bench which would be hearing all their cases for the next 8 weeks or more would be hazardous, if not to the physical health of the old flyover then certainly to the mental health of the municipal officers attending court.

So the pots were quietly removed overnight and milord's flyover was saved from being soiled.

Milord however did not let go of the MCGM until the flyover was scrubbed and cleaned to his satisfaction!

While no one could pin-point the reason for this suo-motu outburst from the junior milord, the gossip at the Bar at that time was that he had become so agitated not only because he considered himself an activist, environment-friendly judge but also because he was related to the renowned engineer who had designed that flyover.

Tongues had wagged then about milord's keen interest in the well-being of that flyover!

A senior counsel had quipped that putting muddy pots on that flyover was like throwing mud on milord's concrete elder brother.

Unforgivable!

Milord later started sitting as a single judge and terrorising unknown juniors while kow-towing to the revered seniors. Newspapers were happy to report his tongue-lashings and pro-active orders.
All those who could afford it,went in appeal.

I happened to be in the Appeal Court when someone sought an urgent circulation in a challenge to one of milord's orders.

Just the mention of his name was magic!
The Division Bench granted immediate ad-interim stay.

Later, after staying several orders, the senior Appeal Court milord remarked in open court when yet another lambast of junior milord was carried in appeal...
"The only thing good in this order is the English!"

That quip still continues to be quoted with glee by members of the Bar.

WHERE THE BUS STOPS

IN *'Milord's Flyover'* I had promised that I would also narrate an anecdote involving the senior milord on that Bench. Here it is.

During that same judicial assignment, the senior milord too started shouting at the MCGM counsel one fine day...

Milord: *"Who decides where to locate bus-stops?*
Do the planners who do it have any sense?
Have you seen where the Mantralaya bus-stop is?
Right next to the traffic signal!
It causes such a traffic jam especially when the offices close and there is a rush of employees going home.
Even we have been delayed from reaching our home many times due to that traffic jam.
Find out who is responsible.

You must take immediate steps to shift the bus-stop at least a hundred metres southwards."

Milord even volunteered to pro-actively assist the planners in selecting the new location for the bus-stop.

Once again, the MCGM top brass felt that discretion was far better than valour, especially in such inconsequential matters.

They soon shifted the bus-stop exactly to where the senior milord had indicated.

Coincidentally, it so transpired that the new location happened to be very close to the gate of the building where milord himself resided!

With the two unusual requests *(about pots on the flyover and shifting of bus-stop)* acceded, the MCGM law-officers had a very pleasant and peaceful assignment in that court for the next eight weeks.
Even thereafter, before these two milords the MCGM's flagship cases always sailed smoothly through all the rough weather.

Long after these events, a senior standing counsel of the MCGM who was also a designated Senior Advocate, happened to bump into the senior milord at the wedding reception of another milord's son.

As they had been good friends at the Bar and known each other since long, the counsel took the liberty of asking the senior milord why he had taken such a keen interest in shifting that Mantralaya bus-stop?

He later shared with us what the senior milord had told him.

It was simply amazing and is worth sharing.

Milord told him: *"You know I belong to a family of famous freedom-fighters. My grandfather too was famous like my father. Members of our family have done so much to serve the nation. Our family name is synonymous with justice.*
I have inculcated the Gandhian principles of 'simple living and high-thinking' in my children as well.
As a result, I insist that my daughter goes to college by public transport even though a car and driver are easily available."

Senior milord continued to talk and senior counsel had no choice but to listen:
"She is a good girl but somehow she was always getting late for her first lecture as she had to walk all the way to that bus-stop.
But you know how I am such a stickler for punctuality. Even though I may reach the courtroom late, I have made it a point to reach my Chamber in time!
This is the discipline one has to inculcate in the next generation."

"Now, thanks to the MCGM's understanding and co-operation, the bus-stop has come right outside our building gate."

Senior Counsel: *"So how exactly does that make any difference to anybody?"*

Milord smiled: *"My daughter can no longer give any excuse for missing the bus!*
And she now manages to reach college on time everyday."

The senior counsel smiled and nodded knowingly.
He realised that considering the dozens of matters where the MCGM had gotten off the hook before the dangerous

Bench headed by this senior milord, shifting a bus-stop was a very small price they had to pay.

We at the Bar don't know where the buck will stop with the Bench.

At least we now know where the bus stops!

As the senior milord grew in seniority *(and insufferability)* the anything-but-collegial collegium decided to offload him on another High Court where his wisdom could be put to better use.

But milord felt slighted. He resorted to the time tested Gandhian principle of *'Satyagraha'* or *'Insistence on Truth'* and resigned.

When last heard he was trying to start a post-resignation career at the Apex Court Bar based on Gandhian principles. Needless to say, it was an uphill task...and there were hardly any takers.

JUDGMENT DAY

AFTER hundreds of man-hours and millions of rupees are spent on litigation, finally a judgment day dawns. It's another matter that a trial court's judgment is not necessarily the conclusion of a trial but quite often the starting point of an appeal or other proceeding in a superior court. There again, after years of labour and toil there dawns a judgment day.

This can go on and on till the judgment is delivered by a court which is not supreme because it is infallible but infallible just because it happens to be considered the final, supreme court.

The most important outcome of any litigation is the judgment.

In this and the next episode I will share some anecdotes about judgments.

Let me start with the day I was approached with an unusual request by a developer from Mumbai who had been my client many years earlier.

Later on, as his dealings became questionable, he had moved on to counsel more tolerant of his kind of dealings.

He would, however, always wish me very politely in the corridors of the Bombay High Court whenever we happened to bump into each other.

This is what my former client had come to meet me for after a long gap spanning several years:

A very senior milord was due to retire in about a month's time.

Milord was at that point of time heading a very busy Division Bench and had reserved several judgments after hearing those cases fully.

This was the case not just with milord's present assignment but with some earlier ones too!

In short, there was a huge backlog of judgments reserved by this about-to-retire milord.

This developer's case had also been reserved for judgment. Both sides had even submitted written arguments to help milord expedite its delivery.

But milord had too much on his plate and too few days left on the Bench to clean the plate.
It was obvious from his anxiety that this developer had invested heavily in the outcome of his case.

So he had come to me with this most unusual request:

Could I read milord's original papers and proceedings and prepare a draft judgment for milord to sign and deliver before he demitted his office?

Observing that I was too stunned by this proposition, the developer quickly slid a blank cheque before me and said that I was free to charge whatever *"judgment drafting fees"* I wanted!

I asked him if the concerned milord was even aware of his proposal?
Imagine my shock when my former client replied that it was milord himself who had endorsed my name!

He told me that around a dozen lawyers who were regularly used for *"drafting judgments"* by milord were already at work round the clock ghost-writing the judgments reserved in other matters which had been heard by that milord.

Therefore, when the developer approached milord to bless him too with a favourable judgment before retiring, milord expressed his desire to help but lamented that he had no "help" available to write it.

All his regular *"helpers"* were already busy *"helping out"!*

At this point, it seems milord asked the developer if he could suggest someone reliable who could be entrusted the job of ghost-writing the judgment.

The developer then started naming all the lawyers who had represented him in his various litigations previously before the BHC.

According to the developer, when he took my name, milord was very happy.

He told the developer that if I would agree to ghost-write this judgment, he could even assign me a few more immediately!

I pushed the blank cheque away and regretted my inability to help this developer (or milord) in this matter.

The developer, not prepared for a negative answer, then took out the senior milord's set of the court record pertaining to his case from a suitcase he was carrying and said it was not a very complicated matter and that he was sure I could read up the written submissions and case-law in that bundle and dictate the judgment in a few hours.

I asked him how he had dared to walk away with this original case-file from milord's chamber and managed to bring it to my office?

He nonchalantly replied that milord's PA and driver were waiting outside in case I agreed and decided to read the papers and dictate the judgment right away!

Alternatively, I could read on that day and he would return the original set back to them before court closed for the day. Then they would all come the next day just to take dictation from me!

This was way too much for me to digest.

I said I would not do such a thing for love or money.
So I may kindly be excused.

Full of righteous indignation I was convinced that I was doing the right thing.

As the developer left my office I asked my office peon to discreetly follow him and see where he went.

My peon reported that the developer had just walked around the corner and got into a white Ambassador car with a red beacon.

The car had a driver and one more man seated inside. The developer had got into the rear seat and they had driven away.

It took me some time to recover from this episode but when I did I decided to confide about it in a good friend who had been on the High Court government pleader's panel for a fairly long time.

My friend was at that time among the probables being talked about for elevation to the Bench directly from the Bar.

My friend heard me out patiently without the slightest hint of any shock or consternation at my disclosures.

He coolly and very matter-of-factly told me that I should

have gratefully accepted the cheque and done the job.

He said that only when senior judges felt that a worthy HC practitioner was fit to become a judge like them, they tested him out by assigning such *"confidential work"* to him.

He then confided that he too had written several judgments for senior sitting milords!

He named another mutual friend who was already doing a commendable job on the Bombay High Court Bench and said that he too had ghost-written several judgments for the collegium judges who finally returned the favour by recommending him for elevation!

Then he named another bar colleague of ours with a huge practice who had joined the Bench as an additional judge and returned to the Bar just before he would have been confirmed as a permanent judge.

My friend said that this colleague too had started out by ghost-writing orders on behalf of *"angootha-chaap" (illiterate)* ministers in statutory appeals before graduating to drafting judgments for the milords of the BHC.

He had stepped down because it was much more lucrative to be at the Bar and ghost-write judgments for many judges than to simply sit on the Bench dictating judgments of your own!

My friend shook his head disappointedly and said that I had let go of a golden opportunity and handsome fees.

When I protested on grounds of the legality and propriety of such an "arrangement", my friend coolly replied that there was nothing illegal in a lawyer being paid by a client for his *"professional services"!*

The realisation then dawned on me that my friend was indeed fit for direct elevation.

No wonder, he was in the zone of consideration. Consideration mattered everywhere.

It seems even the sun shines on a Judgment Day considering the consideration.

JUDGMENT RESERVED

CONTINUING my anecdotes about judgments, I must share with you that a few years ago, I got to know that some of the landmark judgments attributed to a Chief who was an import into Bombay High Court from Delhi were apparently penned by his highly competent associate/court master!

The said gentleman is now a practicing advocate and after a few pegs with friends starts spilling so many beans on the *"Chiefs"* he loyally served that the script of any Bollywood potboiler will pale in comparison to the beans he spills!

According to this *"source",* another import from Delhi High Court used to get his judgments written by the short-listed District Judges who were due for promotion to the Bombay HC.

Apparently this was not to shirk his own responsibility but

to give them *"practice"* for later–somewhat like having to pass the prelims before appearing for the final examination!

There was also a judge who was transferred to the Bombay High Court from Gujarat.

His English was abysmally sub-standard.
He could hardly construct proper sentences in the English language.

Most of his brief orders were incomprehensible.

This judge had founded a law college in his native place which was in a backward area of Saurashtra and prior to his elevation as a judge he had been part of its Governing Council.

His modus operandi in BHC was to reserve judgments in all final hearing matters and push off every fortnight to his native place.

When he returned, he would list all the reserved matters for *"pronouncement of judgments"*.

The rumour was that he carried the case-papers of all those matters with him to his native place and got the law professors of his law college to write the judgments for him!

These rumours attained some credibility because if ten judgments were pronounced on a single day by this milord, each was written in a completely different style!

Even the same words were misspelled in different ways!

But what takes the cake as far as *"judgment writing"* is concerned is the narration I heard not too long ago from a senior solicitor friend whose daughter was interning with a milord who loved being in the news.

This milord was an absolute workaholic and single handedly did the work of at least three milords in any assignment he took on.

He sat in the courtroom way beyond court-working hours.

This milord had devised a unique system of judgment writing.

Unlike the other milords mentioned earlier who outsourced the job to senior lawyers or aspiring subordinates, this milord broke new ground.

He encouraged competent youngsters!

He recruited highly talented final year law students as interns and inter alia, as part of their professional training, asked them to sit in his court, hear arguments of counsel, read the pleadings and submissions and discuss the case with him. Then as per his advice and guidance they were to prepare draft judgments.

All interns worked on all matters.

And all submitted their draft judgments to milord.
Milord then chose the best draft, settled it and dictated it as his judgment!

Apparently, this was how it was done in the USA.

My solicitor friend was truly overjoyed when he showed me an order passed by milord disposing of a notice of motion.

"My daughter has written this!" he exclaimed! *"Imagine. Two respected seniors had argued the case on either side for one full day citing several Supreme Court judgments and this order has been prepared by my daughter who is just a final year law student in GLC!"*

I congratulated the proud father.

He, a senior partner in the a top firm of solicitors, had found nothing unusual or wrong in the milord's methodology for writing judgments.

On the contrary, he was full of praise for such innovative methods of dispensation of justice.

And I did not have the heart to spoil his mood by expressing my reservations about such methods in the Indian context, on that momentous day.

After reading all these tales about the writing of judgments, you may want to know what is my final verdict about all the unusual instances I have set out about judgment writing.

Such things have happened, are happening and will

continue to happen.

When it comes to judgments, should we become judgmental? That is a moot question.

As one of my *"judgment writer"* colleagues has now climbed to the Apex Point of his career, the wisest thing for me to say on this issue is:

"Judgment reserved"

SHEIKH...WHATEVER!

SOME judges of yester-years wrote very readable, memorable judgments.
For them, brevity was truly the soul of wit.

Gradually, judgments started becoming prolix, unreadable and boring.

Therefore, when one came across a judge who wrote well, it was a pleasure to read his/her judgments.

This story is about two judges who wrote really well.
They were sitting together on a Bench assigned final hearing of Criminal Appeals in the Bombay High Court.

The senior judge had risen from the subordinate judiciary and had been a Registrar of BHC before elevation.
The junior judge was a direct appointee from the Bar after having been an Assistant Government Pleader attached to

the Appellate Side Writ Cell of the BHC for many years.
Both judges were very witty and well-read.
Both belonged to minorities.
The senior judge was a Muslim and the junior judge was a Christian.
But temperamentally both were poles apart.
The senior judge was very curt and gruff while the junior judge was most pleasant and jovial.

It was an appeal against conviction.
A husband stood accused of killing his wife due to suspicion of her infidelity.

The defence counsel had picked many holes in the prosecution case and the prosecutor appeared to be unprepared.
This was not unusual in those days.

His singular contribution had been to irritate the senior judge by harping on irrelevant issues instead of meeting and rebutting the defence counsel's contentions.

After about an hour, the judges had had enough.
The senior judge sarcastically thanked the prosecutor for his *"assistance"* and told him to sit down.

As was the senior judge's habit, he straightaway summoned his PA and commenced dictation of the judgement in open court in a loud and clear voice.

The chastised prosecutor thus got an opportunity to open the case-papers for the first time and to go through them minutely with a frown on his face as the judge was dictating the judgment.

Ah! If only he could have done this reading before the hearing!

Now, how can he stop the inevitable?
He knew that the *"dictator"* would flare-up if interrupted while dictating.

Still, he decided to hear every word very carefully and wait for the judge to commit some factual mistake in the narration, so that he could get an opportunity to interrupt him legitimately and redeem some lost prestige.

As the narration reached the point of the jealous husband and his suspicions, the judge remembered Shakespeare.

And he brought Othello into the dictation.
While dealing with the accused husband's feelings, the judge likened him to Othello!

The prosecutor was busy going through all the names of witnesses in the notes of evidence.
He knew he had finally nailed the judge!

Prosecutor: *"I am sorry to interrupt you while dictating My Lord"*

Judge *(visibly irritated)*: *"What do you want?"*

Prosecutor: *"I just heard you mention someone called Othello"*

Judge: *"Yes. What about it?"*

Prosecutor *(with a look of triumph on his face):*
"Milord is making a big mistake.

There is no witness by the name of Othello in this entire paper-book!"

At this, the junior judge burst out laughing and almost fell off his chair.
After regaining composure he said:
"Mr. Prosecutor. We were referring to Shakespeare"

Prosecutor *(pressing his point)*:
*"Pardon me, milords.
But there is no Sheikh...whatever among witnesses either."*

This brought a smile even on the face of the senior judge whose trademark look by default always used to be a scowl.

Senior Judge: *"Thank you for pointing this out to us. Now can we continue our dictation and get this judgment done?"*

Prosecutor: *"I have done my duty milords.
I just wanted you to know that I have read this paper-book very thoroughly. Maybe that Othello and that Sheikh... whatever figured in some other case you heard today."*

A SWEET GESTURE

DIWALI is not just a festival of lights, it is a very sweet festival too.

People express gratitude and exchange greetings and good wishes by gifting boxes of delicious, yummy goodies to those who were good to them, or those who they expect to be good to them.

Practicing lawyers use this festive season to give gifts to the registry staff.

Keeping administrative staff happy is considered the wisest investment because even milords can't pass orders unless the registry puts up papers before them.

Many Diwalis ago, a well-known lawyer who is my good friend had sent the usual mithai boxes to the court masters *(we call them "associates")* of the Bombay High Court.

This, by the way, has now become almost a ritual, especially on part of firms of attorneys.

Lakhs of rupees are invested in such sweet gestures.

To a few *"extra-special"* ones in the registry, who had been especially "co-operative and helpful" in the previous year, my friend had got special golden foil wrapped mithai boxes readied.

I had no idea that there was a goodly amount of hard cash spread at the bottom of the kaju katlis in those boxes with just translucent butter paper separating the sweet stuff from the much sweeter stuff.

I happened to be visiting his Chamber when this lawyer was busy dispatching his office staff on *"mission mithai distribution"*. There were many such mithai boxes to distribute and I noticed that some were wrapped in golden foil.

After his staff left, we sat in his Chambers having coffee and exchanging gossip when the lawyer informed me that each of the boxes wrapped in golden foil had Rs.10,000 in cash stuffed below the kaju katlis!

I was taken aback.

I asked my friend:
"Do the recipients know about the contents of your golden boxes?"

He replied:
"Of course not.

It is meant to be a pleasant surprise for them.
My card however has been affixed on top of the boxes."

I asked him:
"What if they just pass on the box to someone else?"
"You do realise that we are breaking for the Diwali Vacation and registry staff would be getting dozens of mithai boxes from solicitors and advocates.

Obviously, they may just pass on some to their underlings."
"How on earth would they fathom that all boxes have sweets but your golden ones are sweeter?"

My friend suddenly started looking very worried.
He immediately phoned one of the recipients in my presence and said: *"I have just sent you a golden box..."*

Then he screamed: *"Take it back immediately!"*

Turning to me he said:
"I never thought that the boxes could get passed on"

Then he frantically called his office peons and told them to insist that the recipients of golden mithai boxes should put them in their bags and take them home because these contained special *"sweets"* which were meant only for them and their families.

My friend then heaved a sigh of relief.

He was extremely grateful to me for ensuring in the nick of time that his *"baksheesh"* had reached the intended recipients only.

As I mentioned at the start of this story, Diwali is a very sweet festival. But this advocate's sweet gesture could probably have ended on a sour note!

Disclaimer:
I have no idea what the mithai boxes which get piled up during this festive season in the milords' chambers contain.

But I do know that such sweet gestures have always been part of the glorious tradition of our illustrious Bar.

THE GREAT FIBBER

THERE was a designated senior who was a favourite of the Municipal Corporation as a standing senior counsel.

Despite his strange way of pronouncing English words, he was very intelligent and effective.

But he fibbed a lot.

Let us call him the Great Fibber.

As municipal officers often disobeyed court directions and faced contempt notices, this counsel was much in demand with them.

He was their senior counsel not only of first choice but also of last resort.

Attack was his preferred form of defence and most

judges were no match to the various ploys of this seasoned veteran.

One of his pet ploys was to say:
"As your lordship is aware, this point is no longer res integra."

Actually, the point used to be anything but that.
But he knew the psychology of our milords.

They would never admit to ignorance even *(and especially)* about non-existent case law.

Once this counsel had gauged the intellectual level of the Bench he used to throw in random names:

"Lordship knows Ratlam Municipality, Jalgaon Municipal Corporation, NDMC...so many cases.
Everything is so well-settled."

If any opponents dared to ask *"Please give us the citation"* the Great Fibber would look at them condescendingly and retort:

"Send someone to my chamber in the evening to collect the copy"

Milords would smile indulgently at such fairness on his part and imagine he was upholding the highest traditions of the Bar.

The copy of course, like the original, was non-existent.
Sometimes a pesky opponent would insist:

"But the Jalgaon Municipal Corporation case was on a different point altogether."

At this, the Great Fibber would pull out his trump card:

"Go and see the appearances in the law report.

You will find my name there.

I appeared in that case and you are trying to tell their lordships that I am misleading them?"

Then the indignant milords used to give dirty looks to the pesky lawyer who had dared to question the wizard.

He invariably got the contempt notices discharged and the Municipal Corporation was saved on countless occasions. When he passed on, the biggest loss caused was to the Municipal Corporation.

It was almost like being orphaned in the Bombay High Court. But I recall one instance when one meticulous no-nonsense milord heard a matter in which the Great Fibber appeared.

We can call him Justice Strickler.

This studious Milord had his own indexed notebook and was completely updated on most case-law even in those pre-computer days.

Our fibber started as usual:

"Milord may not waste time with such frivolous applications"

Milord: *"We will decide if it is frivolous or not"*

Fibber: *"It is squarely covered"*

Milord: *"What is the citation?"*

Fibber: *"Surely Milord is well aware?"*

Milord: *"Assume I am not aware"*

Fibber: *"I myself had argued that case in the Supreme Court and Milord may take it from me that this is well-settled"*

Milord: *"We would have loved to be there to hear you. But now you can argue again over here for our benefit"*

Fibber: *"I can show you the judgment and save precious time"*

Milord: *"That will be nice. Kindly pass that judgment"*

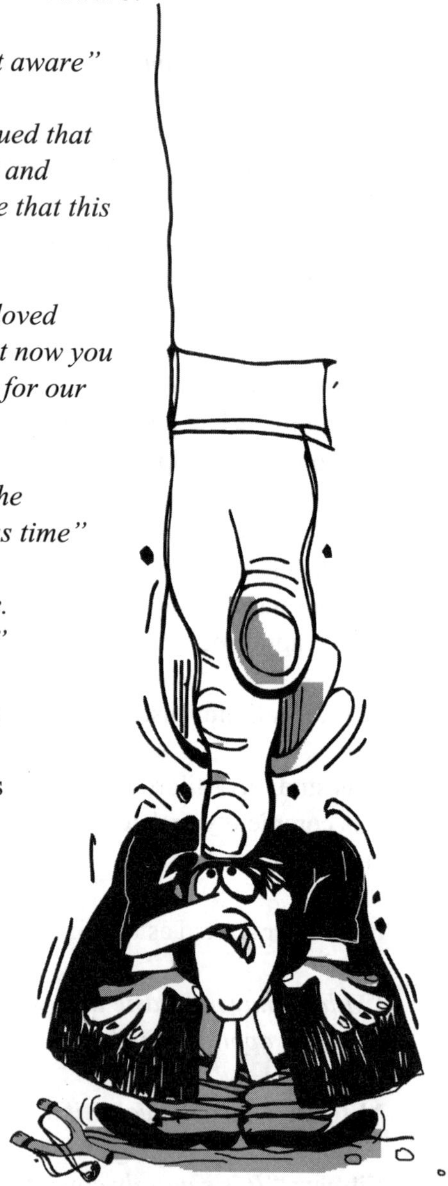

Now, the Great Fibber was in a fix, he started glaring at the juniors and assistants and made a big show of rummaging through the piles of books lying on the huge table in front of arguing counsel pretending to find something.

After a while he said: *"That law-report seems to be misplaced.*

I request Milord to keep this matter next week.
I will come with all the authorities and satisfy Milord"

Milord: *"We will keep it tomorrow.*

Just get that one judgment in the case you argued. Why waste time going through multiple authorities on the same point?"

There was no escape now.
The Great Fibber had met his match.
The matter was adjourned to the next day.

On the next day, a junior informed the court that the Great Fibber was greatly indisposed and the matter may be adjourned by two weeks as he had been advised bed-rest!

Justice Strickler smiled knowingly:

"Assignments are changing after one week.
So unfortunately we will miss being enlightened by that judgment.

But of course we cannot turn down a request on behalf of a senior...and that too on a personal ground.

List after two weeks as per assignment."

After this incident, the Great Fibber scrupulously avoided taking up matters in Justice Strickler's court.

THE KING OF ADJOURNMENTS

ARGUABLY the greatest asset in any litigator's chamber is an *"adjournment specialist."*
I have used the sophisticated phrase we use on the Original Side of the Bombay High Court. On the Appellate Side they are simply called *"date taking juniors"*.

This species is greatly in demand as they cannot proceed beyond that stage.
Therefore they pose no threat to anyone who hires them as junior colleagues. No chance of them running away with their employer's clients and commencing independent practice.

The anecdote I share today is about a very reputed and much sought after counsel whose speciality was to manage an adjournment even in seemingly impossible situations and before hostile milords.

This counsel was a freelancer.
A gun for hire available to anyone who needed his services only for the purpose of seeking adjournments.
Understandably, he was always much in demand.

I still remember that day when he had managed to get an adjournment for a big firm of solicitors in a high-stakes matter specifically fixed for final hearing at the admission stage.

The judge was none other than our redoubtable Justice Irascible.
He had made it clear that no one should seek any adjournment in that case listed for hearing and disposal and the matter would be heard.

Unfortunately, the lead senior counsel for the Petitioners had to rush to the Supreme Court for a day and requested the attorneys to somehow get the matter *"stood over"* to the very next day.

This would not have been difficult in the normal course and any competent junior could have made the request and succeeded in getting that *"accomodation"*.

In such cases typically, opposite sides *"co-operate"* as it is a reciprocal arrangement.
"Professional courtesy" is what it is called.
It is very rewarding.
Once everyone knows that the case is going to be adjourned by consent, every junior counsel makes it a point to attend that ritual and ensure that his appearance gets marked on the roznama.

These *"priests"* have to be paid even if the *"puja"* is postponed because they had all come ready to chant their mantras.

In fact because this case was fixed, they had refused so many other lucrative briefs.
These august values of professional etiquette are not taught in books and law schools.

They are imbibed by devilling in the Chambers of those who have been a part of the glorious tradition of our great Bar.
Some jealous people call the lane next to our High Court *"Fleece Street"* but that is not a proper description.

To get back to the story...
No one was willing to appear before Justice Irascible and ask for one day's adjournment not only because of the stage and the background of the case but more so because Justice Irascible wielded his tongue like a whiplash and would insist on whoever appeared to go on with the matter.

The attorneys were in a big fix.
They realised that only one person could manage it.
The adjournment specialist counsel.
Let's call him *"Taareekh Shah"*.
They went running to his office.

Tareekh Shah heard them out and said it was going to be very difficult because Justice Irascible was a *"No adjournment"* judge.

He had once announced that in his court only death was a valid reason for an adjournment.

Either the lawyer's death, his client's death or the judge's death.

Tareekh however agreed to take on the challenge on one condition: The client must agree to pay him for that date-taking appearance exactly the same fee as would have been marked by the senior who was pushing off to the Supreme Court.
They agreed.
They had no choice.
The stakes were too high and there was no time to get any other top-notch senior ready in a day.

Tareekh Shah smiled.
He said he would have to think and plan very hard throughout the night but yes, tomorrow he would somehow get them a day's accommodation.

Once this match-up of *"Justice Irascible versus Counsel Tareekh Shah"* was finalised, word spread like a forest fire in the Bar Room and Justice Irascible's courtroom was jam-packed the next morning in anticipation.

Milord was about to enter but there was no sign of Tareekh Shah.
He wasn't even responding to phone calls.
The attorneys did not know what to do.
Just then the doorkeeper hollered *"Silence"* and Justice Irascible ascended the dais and assumed his seat.

After some miscellaneous mentioning, the specially fixed matter was called out.
As other counsel gave their appearances, the judge realised that the Petitioner's counsel was missing.
He asked: *"Who is appearing?"*
The attorneys were in a fix.
The other side's counsel volunteered:

"We understand that Mr. Tareekh Shah was to appear today"
The frown on Justice Irascible's face increased.
"Then why is he not here?"

Just then from the back of the crowded courtroom came a panting voice:
"I am here milord, I am here"
Tareekh Shah was sweating profusely.
He appeared totally dishevelled and short of breath.
Justice Irascible asked him to sit down for two minutes and catch his breath before addressing the court.
Tareekh thanked the judge and gladly did so.

After he was on his feet, Justice Irascible asked him:
"What are your instructions?"

Tareekh: *"To go on milord".*

Irascible J. looked surprised.
"Well then, what stops you?"

Tareek: *"My brief is in my car and without it and my notes, I cannot argue"*

Irascible J.: *"Why have you not brought your brief to court?"*

Tareekh said if milord gave him ten minutes to explain, he would explain everything. Though he looked irritated, Justice Irascible was keen to know Tareekh's story.

Tareekh: *"Milord, it is so difficult to get parking. Although I was outside the court building half an hour ago, I could not get parking.*

So I parked right outside the 'Sulabh Shauchalaya'.
As I needed to go to the washroom too and did not want to

go to the Bar Library and be late for this matter, I decided to avail of that public urinal as my car was parked right in front of it."

Irascible J. was getting impatient.
Tareekh continued...
"When I finished my job and came out I noticed that a traffic police towing-van was towing away my car!

I ran after it to retrieve the brief and almost got run over in the bargain.

But I kept chasing the towing-van for half a kilometer to get the brief as I knew that milord had especially fixed the matter for hearing.

Then I noticed the time on my wristwatch and realised that I must turn round and run back to the court if I was to reach here on time.

That is why I was in the state milord found me in a few minutes ago."

By now, Irascible J. was looking bemused.
There was a hint of a smile on his usually sullen face.
"I can keep the case back to enable you to go and get your brief"

Tareekh: *"I am much obliged, milord.*
But it may take some time as I must first find out where the policemen have taken my car.
Only thereafter will I be able to complete all the formalities of paying the fine and getting my car back.
And I am hoping nothing is stolen from it, especially the precious brief. Still, I shall try my level best to get back before milord rises for the day."

Irascible J: *"I cannot keep waiting that long."*

As if on cue, the other counsel helpfully suggested:
"It may be better to place this matter first on board tomorrow".
Tareekh enthusiastically supported this fair submission.

Justice Irascible now had a big smile on his face.
"Will you be conducting this matter tomorrow also, Mr. Shah?" he queried.

Tareekh: *"I would love to milord but I have other important commitments tomorrow.*
However, I shall ensure that someone fully prepared attends and argues tomorrow in my place."

What Justice Irascible told Tareekh Shah after this still resonates in the ears of those who were present:

"As you all know, I never grant any adjournment.
I don't even believe the yarn you have just spun to get this matter adjourned to tomorrow but I am granting your request because of the sheer novelty of the argument for an adjournment.
Matter to stand over to tomorrow"

The attorneys and counsel for all parties happily exited the courtroom. The impossible had happened.
Tareekh Shah had extracted an adjournment from Justice Irascible.

In the corridor everyone showered praise on Tareekh Shah.
He had once again lived up to his reputation.
From that day, he was not just an adjournment specialist.
He was known as the *"King of Adjournments"*

A NOBLE PROFESSION

A few young readers of my anecdotal stories who are just finding their feet in the legal profession told me that they end up getting depressed reading about some of the disclosures I make.

They seem quite desperate to believe that the law is a noble profession and judges are impartiality personified.

Let me assure them that a few warts don't make an entire face ugly.

Beauty lies in the eyes of its beholders and warts can be painlessly removed by laser treatment.

It so happened, as it always happens, that after a few years of struggle, life for any lawyer becomes a bit comfortable.

This is because work gradually starts trickling in.
And usually, it is due to word of mouth publicity.

I was at that phase in my career where I was getting *"second briefs"* to assist designated senior counsel on the Original Side, apart from my direct Appellate Side work.

The case in question involved issues pertaining to the land acquisition laws prevalent then and the counsel whom the client's attorneys had engaged was an acknowledged expert in that field.

I have not come across anyone as dignified, polite and well-mannered as him.

It was a pleasure working on the brief with him, whether in conferences or while preparing drafts to be vetted and *"settled"* by him.

He was a veritable repository of case-law not just on the subject of his expertise, but in constitutional law and excise laws as well.

There was a lot to learn from him.

We had an arguable case and there was a catena of case-law in favour of the points we desired to canvass.

But in the past six months, two high courts had taken a different view altogether. Our counsel was of the view that the contrary viewpoint was equally likely to prevail.

In a pre-hearing conference, our client,
quite naturally queried:

"Sir, whose job is it to show the judgments which are against us?"

Counsel: *"Of course, the other side will point them out."*

The other side in this case was the Municipal Corporation of Greater Bombay ('MCGB'), whose Standing Counsel was a formidable opponent despite being a great fibber.

Our counsel was right when he said the other side would rely on the two judgments which were against the points we were canvassing.

But our client and the attorneys felt we should present our side of the case to the best of our ability and leave the decision to the learned judge who was going to hear the case.

On the day of the hearing, our counsel put up such a fine performance for over an hour that the judge seemed completely ready to allow our petition and grant us the reliefs sought.

We waited with bated breath for the MCGB Counsel to tear into our arguments by relying upon the two recent decisions of other high courts, but imagine our surprise when the compilation handed by the law officer assisting the MCGB Counsel had all the cases on the point except the recent two in their favour!

Even the MCGB's respected senior counsel, who relied heavily on inputs from the law officers assisting him, seemed completely unaware of these recent contrary developments in interpretation of law on the point before the court.

With whatever old cases they had compiled, they argued the case to the best of their ability but the learned judge, who had already been mesmerised by our counsel, an acknowledged expert in that branch of law, was absolutely unmoved.

He summoned his stenographer and began dictating the judgment in our favour. I turned around from my seat and noticed big smiles on the faces of our client and the attorney.

But sitting in the front row of arguing counsel, I could notice that our senior counsel sitting beside me, was far from happy!

He looked at me and whispered:
"We cannot allow the wrong law to be laid down by the Bombay High Court."

Before I could react, he stood up and addressed the judge:
"Milord, please forgive this interruption but this case has not been very properly argued and as a result you may be about to render a decision which would be considered per incuriam if you do not apply your mind to two recent Division Bench judgments on this very point."

Judge: *"I thought you had cited every judgment and argued everything in your favour. I am with you!"*

Counsel: *"Milord, I am referring to two judgments which are against me. I expected the other side to rely on them but unfortunately they seem to have missed these judgments.*

Any decision of our Hon'ble High Court and by milord rendered in ignorance of these judgments will not reflect well upon this august institution.

I am afraid I cannot get myself to be a party to that.

First and foremost I am an officer of the court.

I am not just a mouthpiece for my client."
Everyone was stunned by this declaration.

The judge had a mixture of shock and awe on his face.

The senior counsel of MCGB started looking at his assisting law officer with the look of a tomcat eyeing mice.

Our client had his mouth wide-open, revealing his gold-capped teeth and half-chewed paan.

And our attorney was waiting for the ground beneath his feet to open up and swallow him!

Only our counsel had a serene look on his face.

It was like the look of a Buddha after enlightenment!

Our counsel then asked me to supply copies of the two judgments against us to the learned judge.

He even proffered copies to our opponents! But the senior counsel of MCGB said:
"Just give the citations."

Then looking menacingly at his assistants, he said:

"Let these good-for-nothings do some work at least!"
The case was then kept on the next day to enable the learned judge and our opponents to read the recent judgments and absorb their import.

As soon as we trooped out of the courtroom, our *"Buddha"* counsel blissfully left for his Chambers, leaving our livid client to vent his fury on the attorney and I!

I tried to tell him that what our senior counsel had done was part of a *"noble tradition"* of our Bar.

This incensed our client even more.

Client: *"Tumhara tradition jaaye bhaad mein.*

Meri jeeti hui case haraa dee!

Ye hai tradition?

"Sack him. I don't want him tomorrow.

Get someone else!"

The client did not say anything about me specifically and the attorney requested me to continue as assistant to another senior they would be engaging as counsel that very evening.

But I did not feel comfortable continuing as a player when the captain whom I admired so much had been unceremoniously evicted from the team. So I too returned the brief.

A good friend of mine was quickly drafted to fill in my vacancy as second counsel.
As a result of this case, in the long run I was also blacklisted by that client and that attorney.
On the next day, finding a new set of counsel appearing for the petitioner, the judge must have guessed what had happened.

He proceeded to dismiss the petition but commended the fairness of our counsel and said it was in keeping with the glorious tradition of the Bombay Bar.

For the client too, it did not end too badly.

The new set of counsel advised going in appeal to the Supreme Court, and there, the judgment was reversed and the petitioner succeeded as the Supreme Court relied on the earlier precedents and disagreed with the later ones.

Much later, when I visited his Chambers to meet him, our counsel told me that I should have stayed on in the case as I had a career ahead of me.

I told him that I did what I felt was the right thing to do under those circumstances, and that I would fondly remember this case for what I had learnt from him.

He asked me if I also did direct practice on the Appellate Side and upon getting an affirmative reply, he started directing clients who approached him directly to engage me as his Advocate-on-Record.

We did several matters together in this manner, and not only did I learn several aspects of legal ethics and practice from him but I was well remunerated too!

We still remain good friends, though he has cut down his counsel practice to spend more time abroad with his children and grandchildren.

One of his chamber juniors is now a well-respected judge of the Bombay High Court.

The judge who had heard the case at the High Court went on to become a Supreme Court judge and made a mark for himself before retiring.

He is a busy arbitrator now.

The senior counsel for the MCGB is no more.

The senior counsel who replaced our counsel has retired from active practice.

The junior counsel who replaced me in that matter became a High Court judge and retired not too long ago.

Many things have changed in our profession.

But let me reiterate that I still believe that the legal profession is a truly noble profession, and there is no dearth of ideals to emulate in it.

ACKNOWLEDGEMENTS

Although I am the author of all these **"Tales"**, I acknowledge that I have benefited immensely from the various sources who have provided real grist to my imaginary creative mill.

To all gossipers from the Bar and the Bench
I therefore owe a big debt.
They spill the beans.
I merely water them a bit and allow them to sprout. Thereafter they can be consumed as "health food"!

I thank the Leaflet team: Editor **Arif Parrey**, the first recipient and reader of my products. **Indira Jaising** and **Anand Grover** on whom depends the decision whether to upload my yarns on their portal or not.
I thank them for voting to upload them more often than not.

I acknowledge the encouragement and support given to me always by my three young up-and-coming colleagues and friends:

Adv. Paras Nath Singh,
Advocate-On-Record, Supreme Court of India,

Adv. Sagar A. Rane,
My Junior Colleague &

Adv. Graham Francis,
My Digital Trouble Shooter.

ACKNOWLEDGEMENTS

The illustrator of all my stories is the effervescent **Farzana Cooper** whose illustrations bring my characters to life.
I am fortunate to have her as a collaborator on this book.

Ashwin Borade has been masterful as ever with his layout and design.

Vidyut Shah of M&J Services, Mumbai introduced OakBridge Publications to me.

Vikesh Dhyani and **Priyanka Srivastava** then enthusiastically took charge of publishing the book which you are holding in your hands.

To all my friends,well-wishers and fans of **'Adaalat Antics'** I can only say your positive feedback adds fuel to my fire.

Thanks a lot!

ABOUT THE AUTHOR

Adv. Raju Z. Moray, an alumnus of St. Xaviers College and Government Law College, Bombay is a practicing lawyer.

He was enrolled as an advocate in 1985 and joined the Chambers of Advocate Michael F. Saldanha (Later judge of Bombay & Karnataka High Courts).

For the past 35 years Mr. Moray has been contributing articles and poems to the various publications of the Lawyers Collective.

An anthology of his 'Court Jester' columns for the Lawyer's Collective magazine was published as a book 'COURT JESTER' to critical acclaim in 2017 and a series of 60 poems penned during the lockdown was published as 'THE LOCKED DOWN LAWYER' in 2021.

His highly popular 'Adaalat Antics' stories appear regularly on theleaflet.in web portal.